Further praise for *Resilie*

"To the ever-intriguing realm of
truly distinguished treatise. Deftl
rophysiology, modern child developmental studies, psychoanalytic object
relations theory, and observations from psycho-political arena, Mucci
constructs a sophisticated sociobiological model of hope, faith and grit
that makes it possible for us to survive, if not master, the cruelties of fellow
human beings and the calamities of nature. Her book is a theoretical and
technical addition of great significant to our literature!"
**Salman Akhtar, MD, Professor of Psychiatry, Jefferson Medical College
and Training and Supervising Analyst, Psychoanalytic Center of
Philadelphia**

"Clara Mucci's new book *Resilience and Survival* could not be more timely
and deeply useful in so many parts of out beleaguered world. Tracing the
vulnerability to trauma in individual and social situations, Mucci shows
us how powerfully a psychoanalytic lens can offer productive help and
understanding. The breakdowns and traumas she details come to the individual in the earliest point of human attachment, in all the later stages in
the course of development in the encounters with individuality, sexuality
and social life, and in the terrifying consequences of genocides and mass
assaults on individuals and collectivities. Her book is both a register and
testimony to the suffering trauma brings and a careful presentation of
the social and individual projects for processing and surviving collective
trauma. We need this book to understand the costs of collective cruelty
and social conflict and to design the reparative projects which are necessary for recovery."
**Adrienne Harris, PhD, Faculty and Supervisor, NYU Postdoctoral
Program in Psychotherapy and Psychoanalysis and Faculty and Training
Analyst, Psychoanalytic Institute of Northern California**

"In her latest book, Clara Mucci continues her important exploration of
trauma and resilience based on both her extensive clinical experience and
her mastery and creative use of the literature from psychanalysis, attachment theory and neurobiology. Her categorization of trauma of human

agency at three distinct levels, from developmental and early trauma, to abuse and massive social traumatizations such as war and genocide, and her deft and original explanation of the mechanism of the intergenerational transmission of trauma, lead her to powerful recommendations for how to break the repetitive cycle and heal the traumatized at both the clinical and the societal levels."

Robert A. Paul, Charles Howard Candler Professor of Anthropology and Interdisciplinary Studies, Emory University, Atlanta and practising psychoanalyst, IPA

"In this compact book, Clara Mucci seamlessly integrates a number of clinical and scientific disciplines that are now intensely studying human trauma and resilience. The depth and the breadth of these rich creative chapters is remarkable – from evocative clinical descriptions of a master clinician working right brain to right brain in the therapeutic alliance with traumatized patients, to neurobiologically-informed models of the cultural transmission of trauma over three generations."

Allan Schore, David Gessen School of Medicine, UCLA, author of *Right Brain Psychotherapy and The Development of the Unconscious Mind*

"Few scholars have the breadth, depth and vision Clara Mucci has maintained through her writings on intergenerational trauma and shared collective trauma. Now, with her latest book, *Resilience and Survival: Understanding and Healing Intergenerational Trauma*, Mucci has carried her vision yet further in sparkling and clear ways. The book speaks to readers new to the subject as well as those steeped in knowledge of the range of topics Mucci skillfully covers. Interwoven in this masterful work are core insights from John Bowlby, Sandor Ferenczi and many other gifted voices, helping Mucci articulate a hope for the future where connectedness and deep human listening have the power to offset the ongoing disruptive influences of war, adversity, insecurity and extreme trauma. This is a timely book that our world badly needs – readers will feel a sense of gratitude to Clara Mucci for producing this beautiful, if troubling, yet profoundly human and caring exposition."

Howard Steele, Professor of Psychology, The New School, New York, Co-director of the Center for Attachment Research and founding editor of *Attachment & Human Development*

Clara Mucci

Resilience and Survival

Understanding and Healing Intergenerational Trauma

First published in 2022 by Confer Books, London, an imprint of Confer Ltd.
www.confer.uk.com

Registered office:
Brody House, Strype Street, London E1 7LQ, UK

1 3 5 7 9 10 8 6 4 2

This is a work of nonfiction. Any similarity between the characters and situations within
its pages, and places, persons, or animals living or dead, could be unintentional and
coincidental. Some names and identifying details have been changed or omitted to, in
part, protect the privacy of individuals.

British Library Cataloguing in Publication Data.
A catalogue record for this book is available from the British Library.

ISBN: 978-1-913494-10-0 (paperback)
ISBN: 978-1-913494-11-7 (ebook)

Typeset by Bespoke Publishing Ltd.
Printed in the UK

CONTENTS

I would like to dedicate this work to the three friends
and eminent colleagues I have lost in recent years:
Giovanni Liotti, Philip Bromberg and Dori Laub.

This book is a tribute to their wisdom and knowledge,
laying bare the gratitude I feel towards them
as they continue to sustain me by the faith they
showed in my work.

My endless gratitude and thanks.

ACKNOWLEDGEMENTS

I would like to acknowledge the generosity and help of my young colleagues, Andrea Greco, Andrea Scalabrini, Rosy Esposito and Annalisa Paterna who supported me through the many practical issues I encountered while I was writing this book. Also, sincere thanks to Mary Kane who helped me proofread the chapters of this book, and who was the first to reassure me at the beginning of this solitary writing process.

Thank you to the team at Confer Books: Christina Wipf Perry, Liz Wilson, Emily Wootton and Julie Bennett for their care and attention while putting together this book.

To Allan Schore, Otto Kernberg, Dr. James A. McCoy and Bobby Paul, I give sincere thanks for having always supported my work and for the fun of the discussion of it in crucial moments.

Introduction: Resilience and survival: understanding and healing intergenerationally transmitted trauma

'A latent variable that underlies one's reaction to the state of children today is one's subjective view of human nature. If one believes that humans are naturally violent and individualistic, then one is not surprised that so much violence, aggression and alienation pervades society. However, if one believes that humans are typically not violent but prosocial, one is most likely to view aggression and alienation as indicative of an unbalanced state of affairs that can be remedied. Clearly, we take the latter position.'

(Narvaez et al., 2013, p. 17)

'The history of the evolution of mammals is the history of the evolution of the family.'

(Paul MacLean, 1990)

1 RESILIENCE AT THE LIMITS OF THE HUMAN

Resilience is a term taken from physics, where it indicates the capacity of a material to absorb energy when it is deformed and then release that energy and return to its normal state. Applied to humans, resilience describes the ability of being stretched beyond one's limits and then being able to return to being oneself again, having overcome these difficulties, thanks to our own unexpected inner resources. Resilience defines the human ability to resist adversity and/or to respond to trauma of various intensities (Mucci, 2013, 2018).

Where does the capacity to resist this momentary disturbance come from? And the ability to adjust to new circumstances and then restore good functioning at the physical and mental level after difficult events and to use creative resources that help the adjustment itself? Are these resources provoked and called forth by the challenge itself or are they created in the effort to fight back? Are they innate and dormant in the system or do they become available under extremely stressful circumstances? And why are they not available in all people in the same quantity or quality? Where does this unexpected strength come from? Why do some people experience the most adverse experiences and can keep going, maintaining a healthy attitude and the capacity to care for themselves and others, able to struggle and fight back, while others give way to despair, even suicide, or succumb to cumulative stress and become ill? Can this difference be explained by present scientific data, especially through neurobiological and psychological data, or even from research in trauma studies? What are the contributions of other philosophical, neuroscientific or widely inter-disciplinary fields to these questions? Can they shed light on this mysterious but extraordinary or even unexpected human capacity?

In Auschwitz, Primo Levi called the people who suc-cumbed to the extreme experience of the camps the 'Drowned' or 'Muselmann' (sic), a term actually used by the inmates of the camps to refer to 'the weak, the inept, those doomed to selection' (Levi, 1996, p. 88). The example of the Holocaust has become the epitome of appalling and particularly destructive evidence of human violence and destructiveness, in so far as it is an example of a genocide carefully organized and con-structed over years by a nation state, with the support of the state police, bureaucracy and the silent acquiescence of the surrounding nations, a genocide intentionally and carefully planned by human minds through massive social organiza-tion. At present, it is the only genocide whose psychological and medical consequences have been studied through at least three generations and about which we have a wealth of reports, data and descriptions of clinical cases, with records of intergenerationally transmitted traumatic consequences and research on intergenerational transmission.

The full impact of other genocides in the last century and this one, though equally devastating and traumatic, is still to be fully explored in their intergenerational impact, and have received less clinical attention. For example, we lack, for historical or political reasons, a similar wealth of records, therapeutic reports and studies for the genocides of Armenia, Ruanda, Burundi, Sudan, Cambodia, Indonesia, Latin America, Iraq, Liberia, Sierra Leone, Haiti, Sri Lanka, Tibet or the former Yugoslavia, and for ongoing genocides.

In the Nazi camps, some people died almost immediately, some came back shattered and in very poor health, some committed suicide afterwards. Others, on the contrary, were able to resume their lives, marrying and having children, continuing with their activities and professions successfully, even thriving. The reasons for these differences in the individual response at the intersection between biology and psychology are up to now unknown and somehow difficult to account for. It is also important to understand the reasons for greater resilience, because, if this capacity is not innate, can those characteristics that guarantee a better or healthier response be cultivated and developed? And if there is something in the nature of the traumatic event that makes the difference to the response, how are we going to differentiate between these traumatic events? Finally, under which circumstances can humans rely on some complex psychological qualities at the intersection between what is possessed by the subject (developed or inherited) and what depends on the supposed nature of those external circumstances?

The Holocaust and the extremes reached by other twentieth-century genocides have marked a far point in the capacity for humans to be both inhumane on one side and to confront utter violence and respond to this inhumanity with amazing human and humane qualities on the other, stretching the limits between vulnerability and resilience.

We could say that the limits of being human, in the sense of both inhumanity and the capacities to resist the inhumane with amazing resilience, have been stretched after the Holocaust. These extremes of the human capacity to respond to stressful and violent conditions and to perform violence and destruction require all the tools we presently have at our disposal to understand the limits that the human mind can reach.

In my view, to understand and appreciate the limits and extension of the 'human' means to redefine an area of 'sacredness' in our normal life, a space of trust and hope in ourselves and in the interaction with others, which makes us capable of nurturing life in ourselves and in the other, even after having confronted extreme adverse experiences of the most extreme level. So how are trust and hope in life achieved or maintained emotionally, even in terms of affect regulation and neurobiological correlates?

Subjectivity is considered here through the lens of neurobiology and classical psychoanalytic terminology, such as personality, identification and interpersonal dynamics, therefore mind–body–brain at the interconnection between nature and culture, or biological determinants and cultural and political elements. (For a deeper discussion, see Mucci, 2018.)

I think it is important to start reviewing the connection between the trauma of human agency and the after-effects of interpersonal traumatization, in terms of both neurobiology, and political and societal outcomes. In contrast with the prevailing view of the *Diagnostic and Statistical Manual of Mental Disorders* (DSM), 5th edn (American Psychiatric Association, 2013), which, in all its editions from 1980 onwards, views post-traumatic stress disorder (PTSD) as including both trauma of human agency and natural catastrophes or accidents, I urge a distinction between levels of trauma of human agency (i.e. human responsibility against another human, individual or group) and trauma due to natural catastrophes such as hurricanes or earthquakes or other accidents devoid of destructive intention. As we will see in detail in Chapter 2, I divide the levels of interpersonal traumatization into three levels: the first level corresponds to misattunement between mother and child (or early relational trauma in the sense explained by Allan Schore) (Schore, 1994-2021); the second level with active abuse and maltreatment, creating, in my opinion, identification with the aggressor (as explained in part by Hungarian psychoanalyst Sandor Ferenczi as early as 1932) and with a partially unconscious (not conscious or implicit, as I will explain) identification with an internalized victim/persecutor dyad; and a third level describing collective and massive traumatizations, such as those caused by war, political massive torture and genocide.

The experience of the Nazi concentration camps exemplifies what I have defined as the third level of trauma of human agency (Mucci, 2013), that is, a massive and collective level of interpersonal trauma, testifying to the extremes the human mind can reach in terms of intentional social planning of extermination of other humans.

The levels of trauma of human agency or interpersonal violence create, in my opinion, another set of reflections necessary to clarify and investigate the features of what it means to be 'human' and of the human responsibility in connection to violence and destructiveness, since other primates or other species do not intentionally destroy other groups unless for territorial possession or reproductive reasons. Humans kill for issues of 'race', 'religion' or other abstract, theoretical or ideological reasons (meaning not strictly connected to survival). So what does this essential (it would seem) human intention to enact violence and destruction on others signify about human nature and, by contrast, what does it show about the capacity of human beings to fight and resist adverse events, in the resilient or resistant response in individuals and in societies?

Does a comparison with the capacity to act aggressively and destructively in other animal species, particularly among mammals, help us understand human nature in its extremes, stretching from the capacity to compose the Ninth Symphony to the capacity to exterminate entire populations in the name of a supposed 'purity of the race'?

So, the first set of questions will be aimed at highlighting the 'essence of the human' (whatever that means – we need to elaborate on this point) within the two extremes of utter inhumanity and the incredible capacity to resist or elaborate stress and contrast traumatic effects, going in the direction of creating resilient societies.

In my view, the 'human' cannot be considered an 'essence', with embedded potential for good and evil, but can be defined as a complex interpersonal and sociobiological construct that intersects with deep cultural, social and environmental transactions, starting within the family, the first culturally constructed institution in which the individual happens to be born, in a given historical time, in a certain global geographical and political space. There is no 'human' characteristic *per se* that is not marked from birth by historical, social, individual, institutional and biological features that continuously intervene in the development of that particular individual, within that set of circumstances made of real events, real exchanges, and concrete social and cultural variables.

The capacity to choose and act responsibly in humans is different and does not compare to the range of choice of other beings, including all other high-functioning mammals. We need therefore a comparative understanding of the development of the human mind, in order to comprehend how the human mind is formed. Humans have differences in their capacity for reasoning, in their ability to control their impulses, to make moral choices, to act pro-socially and empathically or, on the contrary, to act violently, to destroy and annihilate, behaving without empathy and compassion or moral values among groups and in society.

If humans have become the cruellest or most destructive species on Earth, capable of destroying the planet itself for our own greed and supposed advantage, but ultimately because of moral blindness and greed, how have the peculiarities of our adaptation and evolution made us what we are? We are a species capable of painting the Sistine Chapel (implying uniquely human higher-order, symbolic, aesthetic, creative and moral faculties) and at the same time we are capable of creating and designing death camps, establishing political torture, genocide and war. No other species can use their higher-order faculties, the same areas of the brain that enable the greatest creative capacities and spiritual forces, to actually plan the extermination and destruction of the planet or the destruction of entire populations. So, if what makes us human and extraordinarily creative and fit for survival of a higher order, and even resilient, is embedded in the same essence that makes us 'inhuman' and utterly destructive, how are we going to define the human? I see all these questions as intertwined and linked to the discourse of both traumatic consequences and resilience.

Traditionally, following Freud's theory of Thanatos competing with Eros (Freud, 1920/1953), aggression is viewed as an innate drive or force in humans, a view also shared by eminent psychoanalytic theorists and clinicians such as Melanie Klein and Otto Kernberg. But other views, in developmental psychoanalysis, affective neuroscience and evolutionary anthropology, consider altruism and social relationality and even justice a sort of evolutionist, preordained development for humans, and violence as a dysfunctional development, or 'attachment gone wrong', to quote Felicity de Zulueta's expression (de Zulueta, 2006). In fact, it would seem that we humans are programmed for altruism, pro-sociality and the care of other humans, as shown in anthropological evolutionist research (see Tomasello, 2019). So, what has happened when aggressiveness predominates? The question is really whether aggressiveness is innate, constitutionally present since the beginning of life, or if it is the product of already traumatic or stressful circumstances that affect the fetus even *in utero*. As highlighted in the inscription at the beginning of this chapter (from *Evolution, Early Experience and Human Development,* 2012), I am choosing this second route of explanation meaning that aggressiveness is not innate.

If in the best developmental route, evolutionarily speaking, we are pre-programmed to be moral, to control negative impulses, to develop frontal and prefrontal areas, resilience is inextricably connected to higher-order faculties that humans can express in the face of adversity. This capacity is not innate but is the product of individual human development and evolution, and also results from the cumulative effects from previous traumata and a different capacity to fight trauma that already results from good or secure attachment and a healthy upbringing.

Resilience also shows the limits of our humanity in terms

of our capacity for creativity and adaptation. However, we cannot separate humanity – or humankind – from its own potential for inhumanity and destructiveness. Inhumanity itself is not innate but epigenetically constructed, that is created, through experience, development and relationships. I will therefore show how our development carries the potential for both, making us the most human and the most in-human and destructive force or species on Earth.

2 THE QUESTIONS OF TRAUMA: TRAUMATIC DEVELOPMENTS AND RESPONSES TO FURTHER CUMULATIVE TRAUMA

Briefly, the reasons for the differences in human development rest not only in genetics but in what we now call epigenetics, meaning that there is not only 'nature' (and biology and genetics) but 'culture' (and environmental features, relationships determining experience and actual expressions of genetics) intervening continuously in the development of a single individual in interaction with others. These 'others' can intervene in the actual upbringing with care, kindness and concern, or with carelessness and potential violence or abuse, so that this interpersonal development is of the utmost importance for the development itself of those human or inhuman qualities, as the practice of attachment demonstrates. Violence and aggression, including antisocial behaviour, are connected to insecure and disorganized attachment. It is the quality of the caregiving, not genetic origin that forms the relationship that the attachment is based on.

This intersubjective field immersed within a cultural network is co-constructed and includes, as neuroscientist, neurobiologist and dynamic psychotherapist Allan Schore has written, not only two minds but two bodies in connection (Schore, 2012). We need another (and usually more than one) to become, for better or worse, who we have become, in terms of identity, affection, cognition and empathic capacities. In my own terms, 'the self is born from the other' (Mucci, 2018), and the bodily construction of the self is the product of the subtle and continual exchanges between our first caregivers and later relationships, creating *implicit* (not only 'internal' as in Bowlby's definition) 'working models'. They are relationally encoded segments of dual experience of self with the other, of which we are not fully aware, but which nevertheless guide our further emotional experience and sense of self in relation to the outside world. They are 'implicit' in the sense that they are working models, relationally and neurobiologically constructed and encoded in the amygdala – especially the right amygdala – in the limbic system. This system in our brain forms the basis of our emotional appreciation of reality at the core of our emotional and bodily based identity. It is the place that connects what we remember and allows recognition of who we are as subjects in relation to the other. Our bodies (and minds) are the result of the complex interventions of the caregivers upon us, influencing, with their care or neglect, the potential genetic patrimony. Epigenetics means that the part of that patrimony we are endowed with is continuously reshaped by environmental and relational interventions, so that what is expressed or silenced genetically depends heavily on experience (two monozygotic twins will express or silence a certain genetic sequence according to the actual experiences they encounter in the environment they are exposed to).

Our first interactions with the environment, starting *in utero*, bear the signs of those interventions, influencing either the expression or silencing of inherited traits. For example, levels of the mother's cortisol in the last three months of gestation equal 80 per cent of the levels of cortisol of the fetus, deeply affecting how the delicate neurobiological and endocrine systems develop or are disrupted. In this way, the first levels of interpersonal traumatization are created, namely early relational trauma, in the case of misattunement between mother and child (Schore, 1994).

Resilience is better understood in relation to traumatic

responses. Trauma of human agency creates hyperarousal and dissociation. This is among the major contributions of Schore's research on early relational trauma (1994, 2001a, 2003a, 2003b) and of Liotti's research, on how disorganization of attachment creates vulnerability to dissociative responses. On the basis of this body of research, I see the majority of dissociative responses in severe psychopathology (as in borderline patients) dependent on this early relational and interpersonal traumatization, moving in the direction of creating a response that *Psychodynamic Diagnostic Manual 2* (PDM2) and *International Classification of Diseases* (ICD)-11 have called (in contrast with the DSM definition of PTSD syndrome (PTSS), *complex* PTSD, in which stress, trauma and pathological destructiveness are the long-term consequences of abusive or dysfunctional relationships.

If the individual has shown resilience in the face of trauma, is the stress response enhanced or reduced by surrounding reassuring relationships, and even buffered by the presence of a caring other? Or is it the presence of secure attachment in the individual that creates the basis for a more resilient response and, if so, what are the features of this mechanism?

From contemporary research on trauma, resilience and attachment, we see that, far from being an inherited capacity, the first element in creating protection against future stressors in the individual, with lower levels of anxiety and reduced levels of hyperarousal of glucocorticoids (the stress hormones including cortisol), is precisely the security of attachment, which is not innate, given at birth once and for all time, but created through a harmonious relationship between a secure parent and their own child.

The fact that attachment is not regulated by innate mechanisms is evident in the fact that a child can develop a secure attachment with one parent and an insecure attachment with another.

Attachment is considered by Schore as the very basis for the creation and development of affect regulation in the child, influencing all steps of maturational development in critical moments in which the intervention of the caregiver is instrumental. Decades of intense interdisciplinary research, including infant research, affective neuroscience, interpersonal neurobiology, psychoanalysis and developmental psychoanalysis, have explained how it is the physical and mental communication between caregiver and child that enables the development of the entire neurobiological, psychic and emotional organism, established and maintained through the various stages of maturation. For Schore, it is based on a right-brain connection between the right hemisphere of the developing child and the right hemisphere of their first caregiver. The same kind of connection regulates the deep or unconscious connection between patient and therapist in the therapeutic exchange (Schore, 2019a).

Our contention here, and the thrust of this book, is that creating a less stressful and traumatic response to life events is possible through building secure attachment, recognized as a major factor in healthy, empathic, mature development. This allows the kind of symbolic, pro-social, moral and altruistic development for which we have been evolutionarily predisposed. We must start therefore with giving the necessary support to caregivers who are struggling. As psychoanalyst John Bowlby would say, a nation that cares about the well-being of its citizens must take care of its families, and be aware that the way we respond to future stress in life is determined by our secure or insecure attachment styles. In fact, our security of attachment creates the nucleus for our capacity to react with less stress, more adaptability and creativity, and allows the use of more resilient responses towards future exposure to trauma and stressful conditions.

For our discussion we can take two paths: showing how security is created, under good environmental conditions, and how the organism in formation or developmentally responds to traumatic stress. I will start with the second path: I think the traumatic circumstances that we are in danger of being exposed to nowadays make understanding and treating or repairing traumatic circumstances a mandatory and urgent

requirement for individuals and societies and for psychoanalysis and psychotherapy in general.

3 TRAUMA OF HUMAN AGENCY

To understand the resilient response, that is, a better
response to trauma, we will need to take into consideration
the elements that make the traumatic event more severe.
Most strikingly, only trauma of human agency with intentional violence (Liotti, 1995), or the impact of a dissociative
parenting style (which impacts the right-brain hemisphere of
the child) (Schore, 1994), leads to dissociative responses. This
includes a vulnerability to future dissociative behaviour due
to disorganized attachment styles (Liotti, 1992, 1995, 2006).
Natural catastrophes do not create dissociation. Dissociation
is considered not only a defence but a structure, the basic
structure of human pathology that corresponds to a fracture
in vertical connectivity in the human mind (Schore, 1994,
2019a). This fracture occurs between the amygdala and other
higher structures in the brain, starting with the orbitofrontal
connections (devoted to planning and control).

Evidently violence and destruction from another being
has the most destructive and long-term consequences on
the human mind. At the basis of the so-called 'social mind'
(Cozolino, 2002) inherent in human development (the fact

that we develop only in relation to another human being who assists and cares for the dependent young in the long phase of development), there is the assumption that the other human will be, in fact, empathic and concerned about my own life and survival or preservation. On the contrary, the extreme effects of trauma of human agency show how, for the victim, violence comes as a shock and a particularly stressful element to elaborate. In Dori Laub's definition (himself a survivor of the Holocaust, a psychiatrist and psychoanalyst who devoted his life to the treatment of other survivors, and founder of the first Archive for Video Testimonies of the Holocaust in the USA, held at Yale University), trauma is cogently defined as 'the break of the empathic dyad'. With trauma of human agency, 'there is no longer a "thou", either outside or inside oneself, a dyad whom we can address. An empathic dyad no longer exists in one's internal world representation' (Laub, 2005a, p. 315).

Another important element in understanding what makes trauma of human agency more severe, and therefore the resilient response towards this kind of traumatization more difficult, is the repetition of the traumatic events in the victim's life, as an after-effect, which evidently gives rise to a cumulative effect that we call 'revictimization'. A second element to consider, in order to understand the particular severity of the traumatic effects, is the distinction between

violence stemming from a stranger (which has compara-
tively less severe effects) and that coming from somebody
who was supposed to take care of the child, as in long-term
abuse or even incest from a caregiver or a sibling (again,
what we call complex PTSD, still not recognized by DSM).
For instance, sexual assault within the family, by someone
who is supposed to be a caregiver, therefore a figure of
attachment, leaves the most severe traces, combining as it
does both physical and psychological damage.

Another element in the severity of the traumatic impact
is indicated by the early age of the victim and the lack of
protection from another adult, who is aware (or should be
aware) of what is happening, so that the person who could
have been a witness is in fact an accomplice (sometimes aware,
but most of the time unaware, in denial or dissociated) so
there is no-one who bears witness to the abuse.

Ferenczi, a contemporary of Freud, who entertained
very different ideas from Freud over trauma, defines this
lack of testimony as a secondary or additional and vicarious
traumatization, due to a lack of support from the environment
(see Ferenczi, 1932a and 1932b on this point, and Mucci,
2013). But even when all of these elements are taken into
account and viewed as important towards the understanding of the elements that impact on or reduce the resilient
response, creating more vulnerability to trauma and stronger

traumatic effects, resilience remains a mysterious, complex human factor and is sometimes demonstrated under unbelievably severe psychological circumstances and in the face of overwhelming physical attack.

I would stress, therefore, that the response to traumatic events is mediated by the 'security of attachment' (Liotti and Farina, 2011) and by the presence of a previously good or bad relational experience of the individual with their primary caregiver. Also, this has a strong impact on future reactions to traumatic experiences, influencing a person's capacity to reduce stress or to amass anxiety and hyperarousal, in turn, impacting on the strength of the self at many levels; self-esteem, sense of safety, capacity to protect oneself and overall future personality characteristics.

If the element of resilience ultimately relies, for an adult, on one's own security of attachment in our formative years, we will need to identify family and cultural or social tools and practices that can help create better security of attachment, a better response to possible traumatization, both from human agency and of natural origin, and ultimately create more resilient human beings and societies.

Since attachment is not innate, it is important to raise awareness, in families and in educational establishments, of how we can support attachment practices and good interpersonal relationships, especially in the early stages of development, the first two or three years of life, and in the second most important developmental phase, adolescence. Individually and collectively, as individuals and societies, we can create 'resilient societies' if we first of all take care of children and their parents. This basic assumption within the psychoanalytic field was expressed and demonstrated by John Bowlby, who first wrote about 'attachment' as a security tool for the child and as the constitutive element in guaranteeing emotional and psychological health in the adult-to-be. It is, in my opinion, a major state and institutional responsibility, reinforced by the family, to make those early years of life and adolescence, in particular, a secure base for future healthy development. This would promote good overall personality functioning, including stable emotional, cognitive and social interpersonal capacities in both individuals and societies.

In this view, one of the aims of this book is to hint at the practices, individually and collectively, underlying the capacity to be resilient and bounce back after trauma. Resilience, in other words, is not a gift of chance or merely the legacy of good genes and the correct intergenerational practices, but can be and needs to be continuously recreated and ensured or installed between one generation and the other, individually and collectively. Also, the fact that having a child rekindles one's own security or insecurity of attachment with one's own parents means that a lot of therapeutic work should

22

be devoted to parents, especially to families at risk, that is, families in which there is violence and abuse between the parents or within the family, including the children, families with a history of alcohol and/or drug abuse, mental illness or even antisocial behaviour (as I will explain and as the adverse childhood experience (ACE) research on 18,000 subjects demonstrates) (Felitti & Anda, 2010).

A major factor in the creation of healthier and more resilient societies will be the reduction of traumatic factors intervening intergenerationally as the remains of intergenerational transmission between one generation and the next. How can we treat, cure, heal and release the stress and the trauma that has been instilled in one generation by war, chronic abuse, violence and domination, and if untreated is repeated intergenerationally and carried through from parents to children? Attachment is also the main vehicle for the transmission of healthy resources or damaged personality features, since a parent who is secure will tend to look after and care for their child, while a parent who is insecure in their own attachment dynamics will tend to repeat the same lack of care, responsiveness, sensitivity and even the unelaborated abuse that they received themselves.

Therefore, a final point of investigation towards the establishment of resilient individuals and societies will be to suggest principles towards therapeutic interventions aimed at resolving trauma once it has been experienced and established as a reduced capacity to fight stress, a masochistic and destructive tendency towards life and relationships, or even a dissociative tendency.

From the theory of trauma, as established by Freud and continued by Ferenczi in the first half of the twentieth century, to the recent understanding of traumatic developments through generations, I will show a psychoanalytic understanding and healing of trauma as the best approach towards a cure of traumatic interpersonal relationships and therefore a particularly strong tool towards resilience.

Most psychological views and studies on resilience, which come largely from cognitive nature and imply biological description, consider resilience as a series of 'traits' in personality structure that seem relevant and can be conducive to a positive outcome. Others investigate resilience as a complex 'process', or a set of features already given in the organism or, on the contrary, deeply influenced by circumstances.

Yet, to my knowledge, a thorough psychodynamic and interdisciplinary investigation of the developmental processes of how humans as individuals, as well as societies, might come to embody and therefore express resilient features under adverse circumstances at a collective/cultural level still remains to be written. This is the aim of this book, or the effort and the direction I take as my challenge, fully aware that my efforts can only be a preliminary view or outline, given the complexity of the topic.

4 RESILIENCE, SURVIVAL AND TRAUMA

Resilience implies resources that are not immediately evident or clear, even to those possessing them. As writer and Holocaust survivor Primo Levi (2017) argued in *The Drowned and the Saved*, the second book he wrote about his own experience of the Holocaust, after *If This is a Man* (known as *Survival in Auschwitz* in the USA), a few years before he died, 'Every human being possesses a reserve of strength whose extent is unknown to him, be it large, small, or non-existent, and only through extreme adversity can we evaluate it' (1996, p. 60).

Do we need to be facing extreme adversity in order to evaluate this reserve of strength, afterwards, in a kind of 'Nachträglichkeit' process (Freud), as psychoanalysis would call it, 'après coup' (Lacan), therefore in terms of belatedness, after the event (Caruth, 2014), or can we try to predict the overall features that eventually can foster it? It should be a fundamental aim of our society to try to strengthen our capacity for resilience, relying on social practices within the family, starting with security of attachment that evidently may become an overall resource that humans can apply to any field of life. Attachment is the main social practice to be cultivated in order to foster a better resilient response to trauma of any kind (of both human and natural causes). In my opinion, the other important social and humane practices for cultivating better resilience are connectedness, memory, testimony and therapeutic strategies for pre-existing trauma. Pre-existing trauma, carried through the dynamics of attachment between parents and children, will be intergenerationally transmitted, if the cycle is not broken through therapeutic interventions.

Survivorship and human resilience

Before we analyse how the dynamics of trauma and dysfunctional attachment make their transmission intergenerational, and before we can shed light on the major practices promoting resilience or preventing vulnerability to trauma, I would like to briefly focus on the very concept of survivorship. I will explore what it means to have survived trauma for the victim, thereby questioning the definition of trauma given by the label of PTSD, unfortunately influencing mainstream knowledge of trauma (inappropriately mixing the trauma of human agency with natural catastrophes) within the fields of psychology and psychiatry.

Why we should include Complex PTSD

Notoriously, the most authoritative diagnostic manual for mental health practitioners in the western world, namely DSM, introduced the diagnostic label of PTSD in the third revised edition of 1980, after the recognition that a great number of Vietnam veterans presented symptoms that could be traced back to their traumatic war experiences. In subsequent revisions of the manual, nevertheless, the category has remained problematic in several respects. Firstly, it creates a sort of normalization (of the damaged received) and at the same time pathologization of the effects of traumatization as though it were an illness, and simply something that deserves a diagnosis, medication and treatment. Second, PTSD comprises, in unclear ways, events that have different origins, namely, trauma of human agency, with its devastating effects on human trust, and trauma from natural catastrophes in which, by contrast, no evil human intention is involved, so that the impact on the psyche and the human devastation are less severe. Finally, it does not include (an omission that has been deemed highly problematic by several clinicians, both cognitivists and psychoanalysts, working on trauma and its effects) complex PTSD, repeated violence and abuse in human relationships, often within the family (such as incest), or outside the family, but always in long-term relationships, which is particularly destructive for the victim because of their human, relational origin.

In addition to this, as it is a statistical manual and therefore does not provide clinical advice or directions for treatment, the DSM does not take into consideration one element that is deemed fundamental towards the actual response, namely cumulative trauma or previous exposure to it, including, most importantly, the presence of security of attachment versus insecure or disorganized attachment in the individual who has later undergone trauma. Security of attachment, with good pre-existing relational bonds, is now considered one of the major protective factors in dealing with trauma. On the contrary, insecure attachment or even disorganized attachment (usually connected with dissociative reactions) is likely to induce more stress, excessive production of glucocorticoids in the neurobiological systems in the face of future traumatic events, contributing to worse after-effects and making healing more difficult. Research data in fact prove that a more negative and less resilient response is associated with the presence of previous trauma, most importantly childhood adversities, especially in the first years of life, from abuse, deprivation, loss or lack of care.

What we learn from the ACE research

Ongoing epidemiological research carried out on 18,000 patients with several organic pathologies such as cardio-vascular disease, metabolic disease, immune system disease, and kidney and liver pathologies, in addition to mental psychopathologies such as depression, addictions of various kinds, suicidal tendencies and personality disorders (conducted jointly by Georgia State University and Emory University (Atlanta, USA), in connection with San Diego University (California)), compared the results of data collected through a questionnaire with an interviewer on adverse childhood events and family dysfunctions. The researchers found that higher levels of trauma in childhood and in the family corresponded to higher levels of disease and mental psychopathologies (Felitti and Anda, 1997; Murphy, Steele et al., 2014).

Let's analyse attachment in closer detail. By attachment we mean a behavioural dynamic typical of mammals (and unique in the extent of the consequences it has on the growth of the human infant, given the very needy state of the new-born) that is set forth in the first months of life for mammals (around seven months of age for humans). The human infant is basically born one year premature in comparison to other animals, primates and mammals, so that the care provided by an adult is of the utmost importance.

Attachment, as described in attachment regulation theory (Schore, 1994), has been indicated as instrumental in the promotion, development and establishment of all the neurobiological and psychological systems, becoming the basic asset and the motor for these systems that turn an infant into a fully fledged human being. From the initial creation of a secure bond between an infant in need of care in order to survive and a (generally) adult caregiver (who is biologically related or simply willing to act as caregiver), all the good functioning regulatory systems of the newborn are co-regulated by the constant attunement between the caregiver and the growing baby, influencing its physical, psychological, emotional, mental and ontological growth.

This co-regulated growth affects cognitive and social capacities, through the communication between the two right-brain hemispheres (of the caregiver and the infant) in connection. The right hemisphere – the analogical, emotional, global hemisphere, which will always remain the hemisphere most connected with the body and our unconscious, implicit functioning – develops and is dominant in the first 18 months of life, in comparison with the left-brain hemisphere, the digital, more sectorial and detail-oriented one, which will become dominant in the majority of humans, and is pre-eminent for language, although the global emotional connotation of the communicative, linguistic capacity, being rooted in bodily communication, will also need good right hemisphere connections.

How can we protect ourselves from the effects of PTSD and complex PTSD?

We also cannot underestimate the contribution of the development of attachment as a protective element in the face of future trauma and resilience. In fact, although secure attachment is not a guarantee of mental health and psychopathology *per se*, it is seen as a developmental construction involving a myriad of influences interacting over time (Sroufe, 1997). Disorganization of attachment is seen as a major factor for future vulnerability towards reacting with more stress to future trauma and a possible basis for dissociation and psychopathology. Research has demonstrated that children with secure histories are more resistant to stress (Pianta et al., 1990), and are more likely to bounce back towards adequate functioning following difficulties (Sroufe et al., 1990). In this view, resilience is seen as a developmental construction within this framework. Children who recover better after experiencing struggles in life have been found to have had either supportive care during the time of recovery, or increased support during recovery. Therefore, it would seem that resilience is not a trait but a process, in which the attachment style plays a large role. On the contrary, there is minimal evidence that children recover because of innate resilience (Sroufe, 1997).

Massive social traumatizations: are they different or similar to child abuse and family trauma?

The Shoah (the Holocaust) and the Vietnam War were two of the massive traumatizations that led to the recognition of PTSD in DSM-III. Numerous studies conducted decades afterwards by western researchers and clinicians have allowed for the gathering of scientific data and clinical writings on the features and qualities of survivorship, not only at the individual level but also at collective and generational levels. The intergenerational consequences of these atrocities have also been investigated and studied. Even though the suffering and the psychological consequences of these atrocities are undeniable, and constitute a warning against future repetitions of those historical circumstances, now 'there is a shift from focusing on survivors' dysfunctioning and maladaptation to their potential resilience and strength, as these children survived the war and its atrocities against all odds' (Barel et al., 2010). The findings, as we will see, show differences and are sometimes controversial (Bar-On et al., 1998; Van Ijzendoorn et al., 2003), but meta-analytic results suggest that intergenerational transmission of Holocaust trauma to the next generation is observed, in particular, in studies with clinical samples (Barocas and Barocas, 1980). According to several studies, signs of the extreme trauma of parents were also displayed in their offspring, even though they had not been directly exposed to trauma. Significantly, they were found to be at risk of developing post-traumatic symptoms (Felsen, 1998; Yehuda et al., 1998) especially under extreme stress conditions (Solomon et al., 1988).

The term 'survivor' is usually preferred in the literature to the term 'victim' because of the negative implications and connotations that the term 'victim' seems to have. We will use the term 'victim' nevertheless throughout the book when we want to stress how, in fact, there has been a real victim–persecutor dynamic and the creation of destructive dynamics for which the persecutors must be held responsible. The term 'survivor' in the book will be used to stress the qualities of the individual who has undergone the violent attack and has come out of it, certainly with extreme pain and suffering, but still capable of seeing and valuing the extremely positive qualities they must have possessed and to which they resorted, in order to go through this trauma and survive.

5 HUMAN RESILIENCE: GENETIC OR ENVIRONMENTAL? THE QUESTION OF THE 'UNIQUELY HUMAN' DEVELOPMENT

In contemporary psychology, resilience is described as stemming from both genetic and environmental conditions. Psychodynamic and developmental mechanisms and neurobiological descriptions of this development can help us to understand and explain where the 'mystery' of a good response to traumatic events comes from. Why are some people totally destroyed by them and others seem to be less affected or to respond with more strength and therefore have a better outcome? What kind of strength did they have to start with? Was it acquired? Can we possibly acquire and reinforce these traits? If so, what do we need to do in order to acquire them? Can resilience, individually and collectively, be 'implemented'?

And furthermore, what makes a human being resilient under apparently similar historical, family and psychological circumstances characterizing these events, which are at least in theory expected to provoke similar neurobiological responses in all subjects? Are there mediating factors for that response and, if so, what are these mediating factors?

Nature and culture, genetics and epigenetics

The nature of that which constitutes the 'biological' in humans is always overloaded with complex, cultural and deeply psychological and existential questions, and yet nobody can negate the vulnerable nature of our bodies as biological bodies constrained in a network of cultural practices that affect our existence as beings in the world and as creatures of meaning (especially in comparison with other animals), belonging to a symbolic world of connections and interrelationships or institutions. Since the traumatized body is both biology and culture, it makes a difference if the biological body has been damaged by nature or if it has been shattered or attacked by cultural (human) causes. When the human body is struck and traumatized by the intervention of another human, causing traumatization, a wider interdisciplinary understanding of what it means to be 'human' becomes necessary, which calls into question a redefinition of the human, in its 'in-human' aspects, when the human has become the agent of devastation for other humans. In the animal kingdom, this does not occur, since domination and predatory drives are simply the expression of survival strategies, not extensions of one's own power or desire to control the other or the environment *per se*.

It would seem that to be human means first and foremost to be connected with other human beings, whom I feel close and similar to, therefore the object of my empathy; then, it means that I see and respect the other as myself, or as my own brother.

When Judith Butler, writing after the devastation of 9/11, a major watershed for western awareness of the global consequences of human actions, posed the question 'What makes for a grievable life?', she was reflecting about death and dying but also, and above all, about the meaning of life as a definition of the human:

> 'We start here [from loss and trauma] not because there is a human condition that is universally shared – this is surely not yet the case. The question that preoccupies me in the light of a recent global violence is, who counts as human? And finally, what makes for a grievable life? Despite our differences in location and history, my guess is that it is possible to appeal to a "we", for all of us have some notion of what it is to have lost somebody.'

(Butler, 2004, p. 22)

And moreover:

> 'Each of us is constituted politically in part by virtue of the social vulnerability of our bodies – as

Introduction

*a site of desire and physical vulnerability ... Loss
and vulnerability seem to follow from our being
socially constituted bodies, attached to others, at
risk of losing those attachments, exposed to others,
at risk of violence by virtue of that exposure.'*

(Butler, 2004, p. 20)

The specificity of the human, not unique to primates but
heightened in humans, is the fundamental social interconnectedness that makes us what we are, creatures who have
developed through interconnection, through the help and
care of another, who create bonds and loving attachments
to sustain each other, whose meaning is created through a
network of social and institutional belonging and whose
very survival is assured by the connectedness itself. (See the
relevance of attachment memories for survivors, e.g. in the
Fortunoff Archive for Video Testimonies at Yale University.)
Our identity is constituted intersubjectively and socially and
our self is born from the other and becomes an identity always
implicated in a practice of 'we-ness'. In other words, this relationally constructed 'we' defines us as social bodies (always
vulnerable) in a network of collective and cultural practices
that both define our vulnerability, make our strength and
uniqueness as a species and mark the site of our resistance
to destruction or our resilience.

This primarily constitutional social interconnectedness is also present in evolutionary anthropological research. For instance, developmental and comparative psychologist Michael Tomasello, who has worked for several years at the Max Planx Institute in Lipsia, defines the exquisite difference between the human primate and other primates as something that evolved from a face-to-face connection, in which the reciprocal gaze and then the exchange of emotions and the creation of joint intentionality created the basis for the evolution that led to the creation of the human ape (Tomasello, 2019). Also, imitative behaviour is much more frequent and important for evolution (see language, for instance) in humans.

Tomasello explains that what is specific in humans, even more than in primates, is constructed of 'joint intentionality', which matures at around nine to twelve months of age and is characterized by a capacity to share attention and intentionality with another. This is followed developmentally when the child matures by a subsequent 'collective intentionality', a capacity to keep in mind others as a group, starting at around the age of three years. All these constructs are developmental features and qualities unique to the human species. These capacities are rooted in the unique motivation present in humans to share emotions with others and to mimic others. According to Tomasello, apes' cognition is mostly individualistic, whereas human infants during their first nine months begin to manifest what he calls a 'revolutionary' desire or motivation to actually be in relation with and respond to the cues of the other. 'The first step is infants' emotion sharing in protoconversations at around two months of age, which evolved as a new way for infants to affiliate and bond with the many adults serving as their caregivers' (Tomasello, 2019, p. 86).

For Tomasello, this capacity to perform or manifest shared intentionality is co-constructed between the infant and the caregiver; it is a kind of in-built human capacity:

> *'The explanatory strategy is* to invoke basic processes of shared intentionality as the ultimate source of human uniqueness. *I conceptualize these ontogenetically as capacities that enter into great ape developmental pathways at the time points indicated (nine months for joint intentionality, and three years for collective intentionality), and, by fundamentally changing the kinds of social experiences individuals may have, and transform it.'*

> (Tomasello, 2019, p.86; author's emphasis)

This different and unique capacity is co-constructed with another human and is not only the result of social learning and experience:

*'It is unlikely that learning and experience play
significant roles in the early ontogeny of this
evolutionary new form of social engagement;
... infants smile and laugh with their caregiver
naturally, thus strengthening their social
bonding without so much learning. Because
infant apes also have affiliative emotions and
direct emotional expressions toward their
caregivers – not just these uniquely human ones
– ontogeny in this case is aptly characterised as a
transformation of the basic great ape pattern.'*

(Tomasello, 2019, p. 86)

Tomasello is certainly right that most of this special human response (e.g. smiling, laughing and even bodily expressions of shame that we do not share with other animals) is programmed within the human system, as is the moral capacity that humans share, with a greater capacity to feel empathy than any other creature on Earth. Yet not enough weight has been attributed in his studies to the actual individual care that each child might or might not receive from caregivers, so that the programmed 'human uniqueness' (of empathy, intelligence, symbolic capacity, etc.) can reveal itself and manifest itself in its full bloom or, on the contrary, is not expressed or reached in the actual development.

According to Tomasello's theory, it would seem that, without exception, children from the age of three have a moral capacity to distinguish between good and bad, to punish, to reward etc., which is certainly true in principle and somehow programmed and co-constructed for each human in whom there is good upbringing. What is not explored in his view is the possibility that human development may be disrupted by traumatic experiences, particularly severe in their effects when they impact a developing being, always destructive of personality and subjectivity.

The findings on disruption of attachment and the study of neuroscientific perspectives on traumatic development show how security or insecurity of attachment can implement, or disrupt and impede, the development of these pre-programmed human capacities, damaging the capacity for social connection, empathy, higher-order intellectual qualities, symbolic processes, creativity and spirituality. In other words, even though we are evolutionarily pre-programmed to become humane, social, empathic and proactive (as well-cared-for children already are by the age of three), these pre-programmed capacities, which are the result of evolutionary growth, are not innate and cannot be taken for granted, because development depends on the actual care those children may or may not receive from another human being who is their caregiver.

41

Resilience, as a complex neurobiological response, characterized by coping strategies and resourcefulness, is one of these features which develop through secure attachment dependent on an upbringing that is caring, constant and tuned-in, resulting also in pro-social behaviour, emotional intelligence and empathy. The first base for resilience is security of attachment, which shows that a child under pressure and stressful conditions has a secure base in their parents or other caregivers, and can ask for their help and protection. Both secure attachment and resilience have at their basis a fundamental layer of trust, hope, high intelligence and self-esteem.

In fact, in Tomasello's ontological theory nothing is said about the possibility that infantile trauma, severe deprivation and other serious misfortune might intervene and destroy these capacities, hampering their fulfilment and even impeding the growth of certain areas in the brain attached to those capacities, with cellular death for instance in the amygdala, as in early trauma and severe deprivation (Schore, 1994, 2003b).

Right now, it is estimated that about 60 per cent of children in the west grow to establish secure attachment and become emotionally and physically healthy human beings and moral individuals (which means, they received good childcare from possibly securely attached parents), even though it seems that younger generations at adolescence already show a consistent decrease of this percentage. As adolescence is the second major window of opportunity and risk in development, it is particularly important that teenagers spend their time constructively with attachment figures at home, in school or in other social, instructive and sport actvities. If only 60 per cent or a decreasing number of adolescents grow to have a secure attachment, it means that the rest of our adolescents develop to become insecure, (preoccupied, dismissive or disorganized), with the potential to become borderline narcissists, or even antisocial, incapable of feeling the humanity of others, whose main aim is to exploit and manipulate others. So how can we develop future adults who can become resilient, assertive, resourceful, emotionally stable and secure, empathic, intelligent and creative, and capable of taking care of themselves and others, including the planet, their own children, animals and other people on Earth? Or if we are aware that these qualities we are aiming for are developmentally created and the fruit of good upbringing, what can we actually do socially to create conditions in which families and children are better supported, and more quality time is available for the relationships of children with their parents and other attachment figures? Or the question is if we really understand the consequences of good primary care, why are we as states, institutions, families and individuals not careful enough? What impedes the actual growth of responsibility towards the consequences of our careless acts and meaningless actions, without considering future generations, and where this irresponsible or even dangerous or criminal behaviour can lead us?

Where are we going?

I will indicate in the psychobiological and social practices of attachment, connectedness, memory, testimony, cultural and educational training in humanistic disciplines and cultures the tools that can lead to empathic involvement. These tools can create a sort of training to feel, recognize and express emotions, with more sensitivity to the best use of the higher-order superior faculties of the brain at work. They are all interpersonal and relational and psychodynamic therapeutic instruments of the kind that can promote sensitivity, care, sensible practices and greater resilience and response to trauma.

I am proposing that resilience is fostered, among other features, by secure attachment. We also know that secure attachment fosters a better capacity to respond to stress, trauma and adversity, and correlates with the capacity to care about others, to take responsibility for our children, our kin and, consequently, to be responsible for our future, including care of the planet and the environment. Clearly, preventing violence, trauma and severe interpersonal stress as much as possible, especially during childhood, would seem to be pivotal. Can we influence this cycle and intervene to put it back on track? It seems that if we help parents and families, we can help interrupt the cycle of violence that is fostered intergenerationally, in turn positively influencing the cycle of how generations become more resilient and respond with less stress and less psychological damage to external stressors.

In this regard, psychoanalysis has stressed the issue of repetition compulsion for conflict issues and emotions that have to be adequately processed and brought to conscience, while attachment has studied the chain of interconnection between the attachment of parents and the attachment of children as a process that shows a correlation of 82 per cent similarity. The attachment style of the parent is the same as the attachment style of the child, with a prediction rate of 82 per cent; it cannot be a genetic feature since attachment may be secure with one parent but insecure with the other (Fonagy et al, 1991).

Also, psychoanalysis has illustrated the dynamics of transferral of trauma through generations, both at an individual level and at collective/societal levels. Simply put, unprocessed emotions, unrecovered memories and dissociated parts of the personality become the deposit that can be transported to the child through right-brain procedures (Schore, 1994–2019a, 2019b; Mucci, 2018). These phenomena are not of a genetic nature, they can be enhanced by neurobiological vulnerabilities but overall are clusters of affect, identifications, fantasies and deposits that become transferred in the relationship of attachment, so that attachment works as the motor of transmittal. All these levels (neurobiological and neuroscientific, psychoanalytic and attachment) are necessary to understand the dynamics implied. They are not only cognitive or conscious since they imply unknown parts of oneself and need to be revealed and uncovered in order to avoid the mechanisms of repetition, identification and transmission from one generation to the next. These processes not only occur between generations but also explain certain mechanisms of repetition and denial in social processes, as I will explain.

The human pact: Trauma of human agency as the first reason for suffering and psychopathology

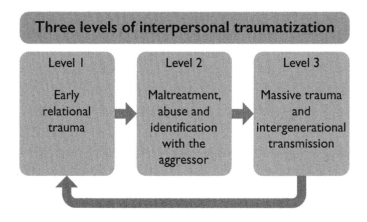

Three levels of interpersonal traumatization

Level 1	Level 2	Level 3
Early relational trauma	Maltreatment, abuse and identification with the aggressor	Massive trauma and intergenerational transmission

Figure 2.1 *The three levels of interpersonal traumatization. Redrawn from Mucci, C. (2018) Borderline Bodies*

Even though there are differences between the various levels of trauma of human agency, from the less severe, namely early relational trauma, to the most severe and huge social trauma such as war and genocide, nevertheless, by grouping all these levels under the same rubric of 'human agency' as opposed to 'natural catastrophes', I intend to stress and underline how the most severe traumatic consequences for human psychological health are due to intentional human violence, not to natural catastrophes or accidental occurrences. In this regard, it is important to try to understand why the relational or interpersonal origin of violence is so difficult for us to bear psychologically, so that it is the main cause of psychopathological development and, furthermore, what the capacity to cause harm to and enact violence on another human says about our human nature.

Also, as already stated, *only trauma of human agency* creates the tendency for dissociation in the child, as explained by Liotti (1995) and Schore (1994) among others. As a disaggregation or fragmentation of the human mind, creating a discontinuity in the states of the self, dissociation has the most destructive consequences for mental health. Dissociation, not really considered by Freud, implies an attack on the human psyche much deeper than the damage created by repression (deemed by Freud as the major cause for psychopathology) (Mucci, 2021).

The fact that there is no clear distinction in any edition of DSM between trauma caused by human agency and that arising from natural catastrophes or accidents obliterates the fundamental element of human responsibility at the basis of the serious disruption created by trauma of human agency. In my mind, it is echoed only by the kind of silence that involves the 'hidden pandemic' of the abuse of children, women and minorities.

The human relational element, which is the fundamental element for development, is also the one that creates the most suffering, damage and disruption when the humane and caring expectations towards the 'humanity' of the other are disattended. Trauma of human agency impacts on our capacity to maintain the positive affects and emotional resources that sustain life (inside, psychically, and outside, in our behaviour and decision-making), hampering the optimal functioning of the systems of resilience, trust, hope, and self-esteem, and disrupting the feeling of connectedness and integration or continuity in the self that ultimately promotes health and well-being individually, in both families and society.

The brain in fact is socially constructed (meaning, through human relationships), as Eisenberg (1995) writes and as Schore has extensively explained (Schore, 1994, 2001a, 2001b, 2002, 2003a, 2003b, 2010, 2012, 2016, 2017, 2019a, 2019b), therefore it is wired for potential optimal social, empathic and intelligent development. But the way the human brain develops will depend on the appropriate and caring response of the environment, first of all on the caring relationships in each individual's upbringing. These experiences can promote the best possible outcomes in terms of ontological development and behaviour, given the genomic input, or the final outcome can be negatively affected or even damaged.

In thirty years of extensive research, Allan Schore has thoroughly explained and described how the human self is created relationally, and how less than optimal care might result in various dysfunctions or deficits in growth and development.

Even misattunement between caregiver and child, without actual maltreatment and abuse, is of the utmost importance for the child's development, leading to affect dysregulation, hyperarousal and even dissociation. The lack of attunement between mother and child, what I call the first level of trauma (Mucci, 2013, 2018; Mucci and Scalabrini, 2021), might cause vulnerability to dissociation because, in the channel of communication between the amygdala of the mother and the child, the dissociative parts and dynamics in her mind can be transferred onto the amygdala of the child. The mother might have dissociative moments, so that the child in those moments cannot be regulated, but is left alone with their own internal chaotic affects (Scalabrini et al, 2020).

Ed Tronick has strikingly demonstrated through the protocol of the 'still face' how even a few moments of disruption in visual and emotional communication, mostly through gaze, visual exchanges, tone of voice and vocalizations between the dyad, can have the most dramatic effects. If the mother's face goes 'still', motionless and without any attempt to communicate, even for a few seconds, interrupting the flow of 'conversation' (what Trevarten has called 'proto-conversation'), the child first tries to attract the mother's attention, then tries to protest with gestures and movements of face and body, then starts crying, protesting at their disappointment for having been abruptly abandoned. We can imagine, when the lack of correspondence is rare or when the disruption of the communication happens frequently, how difficult the relationship becomes and how the child is left alone in their developmental processes (affective, cognitive, social), which require the active participation of the other (for the regulation of the systems and the internalization of the object). A mother who is depressed and interacts very poorly, visually or vocally, leaves the child constantly in this state of lack and deprivation, even though she does not abuse the child. It is the starting place of the so-called 'dead mother complex', as discussed by psychoanalyst André Green (1993; see also Mucci, 2018 for a clinical use of this construct).

We can imagine how severe the consequences of the maltreatment are when the mother or the caregiver is not only non-responsive, or mentally or emotionally 'vacant' (because

she is in an abusive marriage or other traumatic circumstances, is using drugs, grieving or has difficulties of various
kinds), but consciously or actively beats the child, abusing
them physically, psychologically or even sexually (what I have
termed 'second level of trauma of human agency').

Lewis Cozolino (2006, p. 278) writes very clearly:

*'Early interpersonal trauma in the form of
emotional and physical abuse, sexual abuse and
neglect shape the structure and the functioning of
the brain in ways that negatively impact all stages
of social, emotional and intellectual development.
Early trauma, especially in the hands of care-
takers, begins a cascade of effects that result in
complex post-traumatic reactions. The effects
often manifest in what are called personality
disorders and complex PTSD* [still unrecognized
by DSM-5], *which impact many aspects of a
person's functioning and are resistant to change'.*

I agree with Cozolino and have described in my book
Borderline Bodies (Mucci, 2018) cases in which attachment
disorganization or insecurity stemming from early interpersonal trauma have created severe and often borderline
psychopathology and abuse.

In the abused child, dissociative aspects and behaviours or disconnection within one's body, mind and memory, or what Sandor Ferenczi (the Hungarian psychoanalyst, a contemporary of Freud's, who proposed a radical theory of trauma which was very advanced for his time) describes as the 'fragmentation' of the soul through the 'splitting of personality' are present as, paradoxically, a form of resilience/ resistance, a way of remaining alive. Ferenczi describes how the child who has undergone severe abuse survives through splitting with another part of the personality but reacts to life as an automaton. Physical survival is achieved through dissociation in the body and in the mind, with a deadening of both, behaving like an automaton, a response similar to that of the so-called 'Muselmann' [sic] in Auschwitz. In Ferenczi's description of the dynamics of abuse and deadening of the soul, we read:

> *'7 August 1932: Only a very small proportion of the incestuous seduction of children and abuse by persons in charge of them is ever found out, and even then it is mostly hushed up. The child, deeply shaken by the shock of the premature intrusion and by its own effort of adaptation, does not have sufficient strength of judgement to criticize the behaviour of the*

*person of authority. The feeble efforts in this
direction are menacingly repudiated by the
guilty person with brutality or threats, and the
child is accused of lying. Moreover, the child is
intimidated by the threat of the withdrawal of
love, indeed of physical suffering. Soon it begins
to even doubt the reality of its own senses,
or, as more frequently happens,* it withdraws
from the entire conflict-situation by taking
refuge in daydreams and complying with the
demands of waking life, from now on, only
like an automaton … The early-seduced child
adapts itself to the difficult task with the aid of
complete identification with the aggressor.'

(Ferenczi, 1932a, pp. 189-90, author's emphasis)

This splitting of personality is a resource of the individual
for adaptational purposes; it is done at the cost of sacrific-
ing the truth ('they have done that to me') and through the
deadening of the body: not only is reality distorted – the
identification of the self becomes one with the persecutor,
through the identification with the aggressor – but the re-
nunciation applies also to physical bodily sensations with the
disconnection between mind, body and brain. The subject

is an automaton, one of the living dead (not dissimilar from the living dead inhabiting the extermination camps); and the disconnection between truth, reality and mind–body–brain consciousness leads further to alexithymia, a lack of physical sensations, emotions and the impossibility of feeling and speaking about them.

Psychologically, incest and long-term abuse from a family member or an attachment figure disrupts the boundaries of safety and becomes a breach of trust, a betrayal of the assumptions that regulate the care and the protection of the child, which would imply that the other is there for me and for my well-being and to promote my best development, not to exploit me and my body or the affection I can provide (Rachman and Klett, 2015). Several borderline women are often survivors of incest or of severe and continued abuse received from figures of (potential) trust.

In the final level of trauma of human agency in my own description, the third level, both the individual and society are affected at the same time, as in war, genocide, extermination, mass political persecutions, torture, etc., so that in order for there to be reparation after trauma there needs to be practices and dynamics that involve individuals, as well as communities in society.

The thread that links all three levels of traumatizations is the transgression and annihilation of the pact between humans that keeps society safe, the pact of empathy and recognition of the humanity in the other, and this transgression starts with the first 'blow' from one individual to the other. It is well represented by Jean Amery (a philosopher who survived Auschwitz but later took his own life), author of *At the Mind's Limits* (1980). The first blow received by another human being, as in torture, cancels the entire trust in the human order and becomes an irremediable scar in the human spirit:

> 'At this first blow, however, this trust in the world totally breaks down. The other person, opposite whom I exist physically in the world and with whom I can exist only as long as he does not touch my skin surface as border, forces his own corporeality on me on the first blow. He is on me and thereby destroys me. It is like a rape, a sexual act without the consent of one of the two partners …

> 'If no help can be expected, this physical overwhelming by the other then becomes an existential consummation of destruction altogether.

> 'The expectation of help, the certainty of help, is indeed one of the fundamental experiences of human beings, and probably also of animals.'

(Amery, 1980, p. 28)

The human pact

The first blow breaks the human pact of keeping one's own and the other's bodily boundaries safe and violates the inner belief that the other human will be considerate of my humanity and will see my vulnerability, instead of acting as a ferocious enemy. This is the very foundation of human society. Humans as mammals are socially wired towards forming bonds with similar beings and towards the sustenance of solidarity and reciprocity, which supposedly developed for evolutionary aims. As soon as newborns emerge from the womb, they begin looking for connection with the other, showing a pronounced interest in the voice, the face, the breast, the skin and the gaze of the mother. Newborns seek an immediate connection with the one who has given them life (or, with anybody present and available in the environment).

In the same way, young animals seek protection from an older and stronger other and follow them in order to feel safe, setting forth the behaviour that has been called attachment. The attachment figures do not need to be biologically related, provided that they seem protective and sensitive enough: any adult who is stronger and looks protective and responds with care is a potential candidate as an attachment/protective figure. This attachment model (relational, not biological, even if imprinted in mammals within the right environmental conditions) sets the internal working models for the subject's capacity to ask for help in the future, to seek protection if necessary, and to find the best strategies to respond and protect their own young from difficulties. This cycle can become one that fosters and reinforces good connections and social behaviours or, on the contrary, be one that perpetuates abuse and deprivation that leads to violent and destructive behaviours. The long-lasting and most serious consequences are caused by what PDM-2 terms 'complex PTSD' (Lingiardi and McWilliams, 2017), a category including attachment trauma and abuse, for which several authors in the clinical field have asked for PDM recognition, which is still missing (see van der Kolk, 2014).

Ideally, societies should work towards ensuring the establishment of further levels of mental and psychological protection, besides ensuring material and economic safety and development. But violence carried out by nations and collectives, often sanctioned by states or political groups, on the contrary breaks the human pact of solidarity between self and others, so that, instead of providing safety and protection, they break the 'we' pact, the human expectation of acceptance and protection by the other. This pact of care and safety is also at the foundation of human connectedness, namely, there is no self without another and vice versa, as Judith Butler has reminded us with her discussion of what makes for a 'grievable life', since our identity is connected to the living beings who have had a mental place and meaning for us (Butler, 2004) and I have described with the concept of connectedness in my previous work (Mucci, 2013).

As Amery shows, any break in the expectation of the feeling of protection and security that will preserve my life in a community forever damages the trust that the other will keep my life safe. This has been described as the core of trauma by Dori Laub, characterized by 'the rupture of the empathic dyad': the assumption that the other human next to me, not necessarily belonging to my family but just as a fellow of my same human kin, will not harm my life and will instead protect me and come to my aid if I am in need (which is in fact the expectations that are created by secure attachment for the subject, a sort of final gift of having received good parenting). When, as in torture or rape, that fundamental trust is violated, there is almost no going back to this mental place of hope and safety. As survivors often say, they feel they don't belong to the world of humans anymore. The encounter with in-humanity erases hope and trust forever (unless there is social and therapeutic intervention).

To rephrase this concept in psychoanalytic terms, the internal good object, which is the symbolic emotional legacy of good attachment and good child rearing, cannot survive under severe interpersonal or massive traumatization. This is what Dori Laub describes with the expression that, after trauma of this kind, no internal witnessing is possible, there is no other (as there is almost no self) (Laub, 1992). In other words 'the third is dead', in the words of Samuel Gerson (2009).

In severe trauma of human agency or in interpersonal traumatization, subjectivity itself is fragmented (Ferenczi, 1932a) and the personality is split. As a friend, who was raped aged nine, has repeatedly told me: 'Once the mug is broken, you can glue the pieces back together, but the mug will never be whole again. It is a just a collection of pieces glued together.' So, the 'object' is lost and damaged forever. Unity stems from integration and integration has been broken and torn to pieces. It is interesting in this connection that several theories nowadays describe identity and the treatment of personality disorders as a matter of the integration of past trauma with present restoration and the integration of broken pieces of personality.

The restoration (to safety and hope) somehow will have to include that internal and shattered fragility in order for resilience to be born. Resilience will be a gift of tenderness and renewed care experienced and felt in oneself, even for the damaged and shattered parts inside, instead of being refused and rejected by the victim. Fragility, as with pain and mourning, will have to be accepted, embraced and kept with tenderness inside in order to regain a sense of integrity and adaptability to the human realm. It is similar to Sophocles' notion, expressed in his fifth-century BC play *Philoctetes*, where damage is also part of the strength and resilience of the subject, but through a process that makes the traumatized victim first accepted (Neoptolemus wants to save him, whereas Odysseus just wants to use Philoctetes's strength) and then helps the victim regain power and hope and is therefore even capable of forgiving the other. I believe that the restoration process (which we might call 'forgiveness', without any religious overtones) means the full elaboration and letting go of the internalization of the identification with a part of oneself as victim (with guilt and shame) and a part of oneself with an internalized persecutor, filled with rage and aggressiveness, often turned against one self and one's own body (Mucci, 2013).

Moreover, the body keeps the signs and the remaining scars that affected the body and the human fragility, exposing its limits. The flexibility of the body, the softness of human flesh, which make our 'delicate bodies' (remember 'the body's delicate' in *King Lear*?) and our complex and extraordinary mechanism for survival and eventually resilience are also marked by the body's fragility. (In passing, it is interesting that what artificial intelligence developers are currently trying to integrate into robots is a kind of softness similar to the bodily shell of humans, starting with receptors similar to the softness of skin. In addition, the very fragility of the body is also the matrix and site of resilience and resides also paradoxically in the softness and delicacy of the human body, inhabited by pain, mortal threat, and is always potentially prey to other animals.) The robot's 'body' is less fragile, therefore, as it is not rooted or geared towards survival, as we are; our fragility or vulnerability is our strength. Philoctetes is the real hero in the Odyssey, because his vulnerability is his strength, contrary to the shrewdness and Ulysses' use of tricks and his manipulative lying without empathy.

The security of a living being is characterized by the integrity of the flesh as a guardian to the integrity of the soul. In trauma, both have been threatened and severely damaged.

When Amery describes the trauma of torture, he renders or summarizes the fragility of the human essence and the vulnerability of humanity through the image of the human embodiment that makes human life a thing of flesh:

> 'That life is fragile is a truism he has always
> known – and that it can be ended, as Shakespeare
> says, "with a little pin". But only through
> torture did he learn that a living person can be
> transformed so thoroughly into flesh and by that,
> while still alive, be partly made into a prey of
> death.

The human pact

> 'Whoever has succumbed to torture can no
> longer feel at home in the world. The shame of
> destruction cannot be erased. Trust in the world,
> which already collapsed in part at the first blow,
> but in the end, under torture, fully, will not be
> regained. That one's fellow man was experienced
> as the anti-man remains in the tortured person
> as accumulated horror. It blocks the view into a
> world in which the principle of hope rules.'
>
> (Amery, 1980, p. 40)

When trust and hope are erased and eradicated, the human spirit is dead. Humans become mere bodies reduced to unconscious survival. Their vulnerability is totally exposed and unredeemable. And yet, the frailty of the body (and of the emotional life) is one with its potential for resilience and restoration and cure (in the body) and its fragility resides in the very humanity and empathic source of our being human, resulting in final resilience.

The 'Muselmann' in Primo Levi's description is one who has lost trust and hope and is reduced to flesh in an already dead soul, as sheer 'mortal coil', in Hamlet's words, the bare body essence that does not define the human but is a biological shell that we share with other mammals.

CONSEQUENCES OF THE THREE LEVELS OF TRAUMA OF HUMAN AGENCY AND HOW THEY AFFECT RESILIENCE

In all levels of trauma of human agency, at the neurobiological level there will be consequences: first, hyperarousal, with high levels of stress and glucocorticoids, including cortisol in excess, and the possible dissociative structure at the basis of further destructive behaviour and psychopathology. We should remember the cumulative effects of certain elements, such as the underlying attachment style, the age of the victim (the earlier the trauma, the more destructive), duration, frequency and extreme features, such as bizarre behaviour and motivations, and other elements linked to the power-lessness of the victim and the meaning that the victim and their culture attach to the traumatic events.

To better understand the consequences, the first level of trauma ('early relational trauma' according to Schore, 1994) is caused by the lack of good attunement between mother and child, following Allan Schore's interdisciplinary and ground-breaking research carried out over the last thirty years (from the first monumental volume in 1994 to the last two books, which appeared in 2019). In this case, the caregiver, because of psychopathology, previous and present stress or trauma, use of drugs, depression, severe loss and other serious difficulties, cannot give the best level of care that the child requires for optimal development, creating affect dysregulation, hyperarousal and possible dissociation, and a high level of glucocorticoids on the hypothalamic–pituitary–adrenal axis (HPA), which in turn affects the immune system. (This is currently widely debated when the healthy functioning of the immune system is deemed essential to fight the COVID-19 coronavirus and other possible future epidemics.) In terms of psychopathological effects and symptoms, affect dysregulation (incapacity to control fear, rage and anger) might result in dangerous behaviours such as drug and alcohol abuse, eating disorders, especially obesity and bulimia (where food is used as an affect regulator), and dependent behaviours in relationships, besides impulsivity and lack of control. It also implies amygdala activation without control of higher areas of the brain, in the orbitofrontal and frontal areas (Schore, 1994) which is typical of the functioning of borderline personality disorders.

The second level (in combination with the first level, lack of attunement) adds to the first level (involving *non*-intentional misattunement of the caregiver) the additional stress and dynamic consequences of severe abuse or maltreatment and severe deprivation, which are deemed the causes of vulnerability towards developing disorganized attachment in the child and possible dissociative behaviours.

This level is particularly visible in the destructive features of personality disorders, in addition to the dysregulation and impulsivity present as a consequence of the first level, because (and this is my own contribution following the identification with the aggressor as explained by Sandor Ferenczi) it creates a split in the personality, a dissociated and internalized dyad with a part of oneself as victim identified with the victim's affects (low self-esteem, blame, shame, guilt) and a part of oneself identified with an internal persecutor of which the subject is not aware, identified with the affects of the persecutor (violence, hate, aggressiveness – often revolved around one's own body).

An identification with the aggressor (Ferenczi, 1932a and 1932b) is used by the personality to adapt in order to survive. The internalized persecutory parts can act against oneself (damaging oneself and one's resources) or against the other (becoming actually violent against another). I have also assimilated this internalization of a persecutor of traumatic violent origin to the formation of the alien self, as explained by Bateman and Fonagy (2004), but in my view this alien self that is then externalized through violent behaviour and destructiveness is really due not only to lack of mirroring between mother and child (as in Fonagy's theory), but also to the real hate and hostility that the mother has felt and directed against the child. This is a concept that Ferenczi

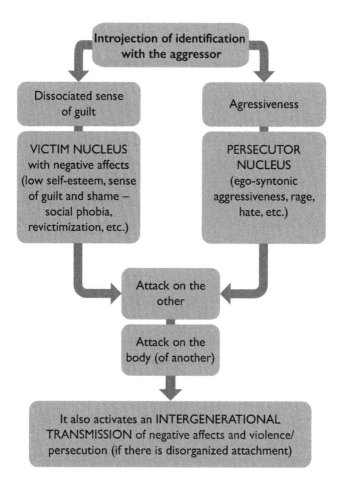

Figure 2.2 *Introjection of identification with the aggressor.*
Redrawn from Mucci, 2018

referred to as the complex of the 'ill-received child' (Ferenczi, 1929), which creates destruction and a death drive in the future adult. Important in a rewriting of some of the tenets of psychoanalytic theory, it is evident here how the origin of the death drive is, for Ferenczi, not innate or originated by mere chance, but the result of an original rejection of and violence enacted on the child, on behalf of the parents or caregivers, in contrast with Freud's theorization.

Regarding the internalization of violence in the victim and the subsequent externalization, the male victim more often becomes a persecutor (of other victims) in patriarchal and masculinist societies, where aggressiveness is considered more acceptable in male children, so that the identification with the aggressor becomes internalized aggressiveness in the male child/adolescent/adult and is more often directed against the other. The abused female child more often directs that received and internalized aggressiveness against herself, her children or her own body (in a reversal of the dynamics that often lead to depression and self-harm and sometimes also to suicidal tendencies). In fact, 80 per cent of borderline patients who self-harm and feel suicidal are female; males seem, as far as diagnosis is concerned, to be more often narcissistic or antisocial, with ego-syntonic aggressiveness.

We can see very clearly this typical victim/persecutor split at work in severe personality disorders, that are so common, especially in young adults nowadays. Borderline patients cut themselves or try to commit suicide; severe narcissists damage their own resources (including time and intelligence) in order to protect, through the defence of grandiosity and omnipotent control, their own inner fragility and low self-esteem, and can also become malignant narcissists (a clinical diagnosis not present in DSM but described by Otto Kernberg, 1975). They behave disruptively against common rules shared by others and implemented by institutions, towards which they feel a sense of entitlement that makes them act beyond the normal constrictions that affect others in society.

Research shows more and more consistently how subjects affected by personality disorders have been exposed to levels of traumatizations[1] that sometimes are not consciously recognized as traumatic events because of the dissociation accompanying their personalities and their symptoms, especially when trauma involves attachment relationships, or long-term relationships, creating the symptoms of 'complex PTSD'. Their psychopathology is expressed through symptoms and destructiveness in various aspects of their lives. Gabbard reports in *Psychodynamic Psychiatry* that 60 per cent

---

[1] The traumatic origin of personality disorders is a very controversial issue, difficult to prove through research but filled with clinical truth. It is the major thesis of *Borderline Bodies* (Mucci, 2018) and evident in my personal experience with clinical work with borderline personality disorders.

of borderline patients have been victims of sexual abuse. Paris, Gunderson, Zanarini, Fonagy, Liotti and other major experts and clinicians on borderline disorders see, in the typically split identity and the consequent destructive behaviours of these patients, a sign of trauma of human agency.

Finally, the massive traumatizations created by war, genocide, political regimes inflicting torture and atrocities on civilian populations leave severe symptoms in the first generation (as depression, alexithymia and anhedonia, muscular and bone pain, insomnia and nightmares), with aspects of denial and dissociation. But these traumata also create symptoms in the second and third generations of survivors, with the maximum negative effect on the third generations, if the traumatic origin is not elaborated and appropriately healed, as Lifton, Krystal, Kestenberg and many others have explained. Often survivors themselves, these authors have analysed in depth the symptoms of the first generation and the dynamics of transpositions of trauma through future generations (for a synthetic overview and a discussion, see Mucci, 2008, 2013).

Let me stress here that although the first two levels of traumatizations are very often at the basis of the dynamics shown in their destructiveness by people with personality disorders (see Mucci, 2018), the third level is *not per se* conducive to personality disorders but might result in a difficulty in child rearing, therefore we go back to the first and/or second level of traumatization, for the second generation.

In fact, parents who have undergone massive traumatization might not be in the best state for the particular attunement and enormous physical and especially emotional work of looking after offspring, so that they might become uncaring or even abusive parents, with lack of emotional attunement, or even manifest abuse or depriving behaviour, that describes the first and second levels of traumatization. If we think of the masses of persecuted, displaced and traumatized people who are currently trying to emigrate, fleeing war zones, or racial or religious persecution, or trying to relocate to areas of the planet with better land or improved living conditions, we can imagine the levels of intergenerational transmission that we are going to face through the next decades, together with the additional problem of overpopulated countries and not enough resources (since 20 per cent of the wealthiest people consume 80 per cent of the global resources), if we do not try to understand, alleviate and heal the traumatizations of these parents.

3

Attachment: An interpersonal vehicle of transmission and mediation of trauma

In the struggle towards survival, the neurobiological effects of trauma are mediated by secure or insecure attachment, contributing to the raising or downregulating of the level of stress hormones (glucocorticoids and cortisol especially), creating a further positive or negative impact on the destructive experience. The attachment system works as a buffer (in the case of secure attachment) or as an amplifier of the stress. In other words, the person who has experienced trauma of the first or second level will react with more stress, more anxiety, more neurobiological disruption to the further traumatizations of human origin, or of natural or accidental origin.

Psychodynamically, secure attachment in the child (and therefore between at least one parent and the child) works as a protection towards future traumatization, because of the internalization of a good parental image, a soothing, internalized good object, which might regulate negative emotions and cushion feelings of helplessness and loneliness that are at the core of any psychic traumatization allowing also affect regulation of the negative emotions.

THE NEUROBIOLOGICAL ADVANTAGE OF SECURE ATTACHMENT FOR MENTAL AND PHYSICAL HEALTH AND WELL-BEING

As Narvaez et al. (2013, p.5) argue:

> '[T]he healthy integration of the lower primary process emotional affective powers of the mind and the emergent secondary (learning) and tertiary (thoughtful) cognitive landscape are left to environmental influences, especially to families and to the surrounding cultural milieus.'

Sensitive periods of maturation for emotional, social and cognitive functioning (Nelson and Panksepp, 1998) have been identified by developmental neuroscience. These periods are genetically set but can be reinforced or depleted in the interaction with a stimulating or deprived environment. Clearly, environment can contribute to optimal development but also to less than optimal development where traumatic events have occurred.

We have to resort to animal research and models to develop parameters to understand growth and development in the human realm. There seem to be enormous similarities, especially for the subcortical (amygdala, limbic system, affective systems) substrate and the biochemicals regulating them, orchestrating the functioning of emotional and motivational substrates and their responses. Those systems, namely the limbic connections with the higher areas that are determinant for the control of impulses and for planning our actions at individual and social levels, develop in a fulfilling dyadic relationship and, even if genetically imprinted, are epigenetically (environmentally, through relationships of growth and care) reinforced.

Compared with other animals, humans, as we have already noted, have to be reared until they reach the capacity to further develop and use the higher areas of the brain. At birth, only 23 per cent of the human brain is formed (Sapolsky, 2017). The higher areas are hierarchically developed in stages in an integrated way, from lower to higher. Only humans have the higher symbolic representations of a reality outside of them, of their own estimate of the experience that leaves an imprint, biological and affective at first, finally achieving (but only if certain maturational levels are reached) the exquisite development of higher order faculties with the potential for control, planning and deferral of action for higher benefit,

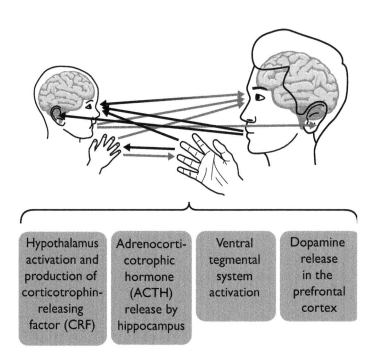

Figure 3.1 *Attachment development.*
Redrawn from Mucci, C. (2018) Borderline Bodies

including moral choices. (By moral choice, I mean the capacity to discriminate and choose the best for oneself and for others at a higher ethical and altruistic level, or a level of choice that considers the benefit to others in connection with oneself.) At the same time, the very capacity to control and respond morally in a highly creative and beneficial way can be disrupted by upbringing and become impaired. So the human potential for good that is deposited in the higher levels of human faculties (which is not found in other primates and mammals) is nonetheless what might determine the lack of empathy and the subsequent levels of indifference or even the will to harm the other, so that we could conclude, as the Latin saying goes, that *'corruptio optimi pessima'*: the impairment of the potentially best leads to the worst outcome.

Development at all hierarchical levels – from the lowest or earlier and more primitive development, to the highest, and further or more advanced – is regulated through the consistent interaction with another being, an adult who interacts and constantly contributes, through care, love, protection and appropriate modulation of behaviour, to make the environment a nurturing place for the child's expression and growth. Or who, on the contrary, might make the relationship a place of conflict, deprivation, neglect and abuse.

The regulatory systems that help the functioning of all neurobiological circuits are largely dyadic (Tronick, 2007). In particular, it is important to consider that the appropriate attunement between parent and child, especially during sensitive periods of development, can contribute to that development in a positive way and that, in the absence of such attunement, development can be impeded in the following ways:

1. The growth of neurites (the nerve endings of cells) that extend in localised regions or distribute themselves in different areas.
2. The creation of new or wider synapses (that allow communication across areas and systems).
3. The formation, along the axons, of the myelin sheet, which speeds up the conduction of electric signals, making the connection quicker.
4. Changes at the level of the post-synaptic membrane of the receiving cells, determining cellular death phenomena, due to insufficient usage or degenerative processes (such as chronic stress; as happens to the amygdala).

Barnes et al. (1995), Kempermann et al. (1997) and Hockfield and Lombroso (1998) have demonstrated in their experiments on animals that particularly stimulating environments are associated with a greater density of synaptic stimulation, with an increase in the number of neurons, and in the volume of the hippocampus, a fundamental region for learning and memory. Therefore, even if the genetic component remains essential, experience becomes decisive for the development of the brain, because what is finally expressed of the genetic possibilities depends on the quality of the relationship and the appropriate stimulation provided by the environment. Touch, voice, eye contact, care and appropriate tuning and a not-too-long disruption in the dis-attunement of the dyad are all necessary tools for the dyad to work properly. It is likely that mental organization proceeds through the gradual increase of the neuronal connections, until a critical point is reached in which a superior organization emerges spontaneously (Edelman, 1987; Maffei, 2011).

Dissociation, not repression, is caused by trauma of human agency

It is now widely acknowledged that severe psychopathology has at its roots dissociation (always of traumatic origin) and not repression, as was maintained by Freudian psychoanalysis (see Mucci, 2021; Schore, 1994, 2001b, 2003a, 2003b).

More than a defence mechanism, we now consider dissociation as a developmental structure, a vertical interruption of connection, a disintegration of the sense of the self finally involving several levels of detachment, of consciousness and splitting. A typical example of severe dissociation is that of a patient who, in describing her abuse at the hands of a relative, speaks of herself as if she were watching the whole scene from the ceiling of the room, outside of her own body (speaking almost completely in the third person). She describes a child being abused by an adult in the room below her. In her consciousness, levels of dissociation and denial are compounded so that: first, that is not my body (depersonalization, a level of dissociation regarding one's body: it is not mine); second, that is not my uncle/father/etc. (denial); this is not happening to me (denial of the reality of the event). All these splits are necessary to prevent one's consciousness from acknowledging the reality of it ('I have been abused'); the responsibility of the adult (often an attachment figure, which makes the break in trust even more severe): 'he is the aggressor; he is responsible for it'; the actual physical impression resulting from the abuse: rage, disgust, fear, and other feelings or physical sensations further confusing the victim.

The body becomes the disregarded culprit; it is the body that feels disgust, rage, self-loathing, and other sensations, but it is impossible to connect those feelings to the self, since the self has been physically, emotionally and cognitively disconnected. Ferenczi was among the first psychoanalysts to acknowledge how sexual abuse of a child, in particular when inflicted by a relative (in all cases of incest but even more so when the caregiver is the perpetrator), creates a 'splitting of personality' (Ferenczi, 1932a). This was in the 1930s, decades before the connection between trauma and personality disorders was made, and before the very term and possible condition that we now define as 'borderline disorder' even existed. Philip Bromberg's definition of dissociation clarifies why dissociation as a mechanism is put forth in order for the child to maintain a sense of continuity of the self, following the destabilizing behaviour of the caregiver:

> 'In order to preserve the attachment connection
> and protect mental stability, the mind triggers
> a survival solution, dissociation, that allows
> the person to bypass the mentally disorganizing
> struggle to self-respect without hope of relieving
> the pain and fear caused by the destabilization
> of selfhood. Dissociation narrows one's range of
> perception so as to set up non-conflictual categories
> of self-experience as different parts of the self.'

(Bromberg, 2011, p. 43)

The link between denial and defensive dissociation (becoming an organizing structure of the mind, deleting pieces of reality in simultaneous contrast), is clearly expressed by Bromberg:

> 'When functioning as a mental structure,
> dissociation controls potentially traumatic

*experience by turning each domain of self into a
discontinuous constellation of reality now kept
aside from others by the auto-hypnotic process
that supports dissociation. Defensive dissociation
shows its signature through disconnecting the
mind from its capacity to perceive that which feels
too much for selfhood to bear. It reduces what is
in front of someone's eyes to a narrow band of
perceptual reality that lacks emotionally personal
relevance to the self that is experiencing it
("whatever is going on is not happening to me").*

(Bromberg, 2011, p. 50)

Very cogently, Bromberg views dissociation as a reaction or a defence to trauma arising from human relationships, whereas repression is 'responsive to anxiety' (2011, p. 49).

The fact that only trauma of human agency creates dissociation in the psyche, as Liotti, from a cognitivist point of view, and Schore, from a wider interdisciplinary angle, argue, points at the utmost importance for the human psyche to create and maintain a bond with the other, a bond based on trust and security. It also explains why Laub speaks of interpersonal trauma as the rupture of the empathic dyad. And it points to the fact that children would rather view themselves as guilty or bad rather than accuse the parent of harmful conduct and, if forced to choose, would rather be with the parent than separated from that bond, as though a bond, even a negative one, is better than no bond and no connection at all. As Ferenczi writes as early as 1932, the patient thinks: 'it cannot be true that this is happening to me, or someone would come to my aid' (Ferenczi, 1932a, p. 25).

Ferenczi adds: [As a consequence of trauma and abuse] 'The child is helpless and confused, should she struggle to prevail over the will of adult authority, the disbelief of her mother, etc. Naturally she cannot do that, she is faced with the choice – is it the world that is bad or am I wrong? – and chooses the latter' (Ferenczi, 1932, p. 80).

Giovanni Liotti, a specialist in attachment and cognitivist psychotherapy, who has written extensively on child abuse and the traumatic basis of the vulnerability to dissociation and other levels of psychopathology, describes dissociation as a discontinuity of consciousness and defines several levels of detachment from consciousness, namely absorption, depersonalization, derealization, amnesia, and other forms of disconnection between consciousness and experience, mind and body, evident in the patient's behaviour.

In children, only abuse and insecure or disorganized attachment can create dissociation. Therefore, if a child is dissociated after, for instance, an earthquake, it depends on

the insecurity or even disorganization of attachment between that child and its caregiver, who evidently because
of their (the parent's) own problems unfortunately has not
been able to protect the child adequately from the event. In
other words, their relationship is not strong, stable and reliable enough to work as a secure base for the child towards
external events, and this is very likely because the parents
themselves do not have secure attachment. Because of this
lack of secure attachment between mother and child, the
latter remains in a traumatized state for an excessive period
of time. The child is left alone, without proper attunement
and affect regulation, to cope with internal states of anxiety
and fear and other negative affects. The child needs another
to down-regulate them and to internalize the mechanism
of regulation that needs to be learned through another who
has done that extensively with the child. It is necessary that
the child, through the other, elaborates the mechanism of
projective identification that would allow them to process
and digest the traumatic events without a filter (what Bion
called 'reverie', the containment and elaboration of affect that
a child cannot do alone, and what for Green creates what he
terms the 'dead mother complex' (Green, 1993), meaning a
mother psychically dead for the child).

Dissociation becomes a structuring model of response
to future trauma in children who have undergone abuse and

severe misattunement between parent and child, or also have had parents who have undergone extreme traumatizations, as in the Holocaust and other genocides. In the case of dissociation caused by the third level of traumatizations (massive social trauma as in genocides and war), this traumatic extreme experience can obviously be transmitted, as a structure stemming not from abuse from the traumatized parent but probably from the deprivation and the alexithymic response of the parent who suffers from dissociation and unelaborated pain and mourning.

It should also be noted that most violent and abusive behaviours are performed in dissociative/denial states by the parent/perpetrator. The most relevant of these is probably incest, where the truth of what is inflicted on the child is continuously negated, denied, dissociated by the perpetrator and probably goes hand in hand with previous traumatic experiences in the abusers themselves, which have left in them dissociative states in which they literally become the persecutors (enacting the other part of the victim–persecutor dyad that they have internalized, unconsciously, and that is unconsciously enacted in a dissociative modality, often without the possibility of even remembering the misdeeds). I am saying this in no redemption or condoning of their acts but really with the aim of describing the psychodynamics of repetition that might indeed have at their basis a traumatic origin, therefore repeating a cycle of abuse and victimization that needs to be stopped.

Another origin of violence therefore would be reduced if the dissociative patterns (always linked to trauma, never innate or the fruit of DNA) could be recognized, analysed in therapy and healed. Abuse of children, including incest, is very probably a way of releasing stress in an unconscious/dissociated/negated way.

Why do parents and other adults abuse?

The development of an attachment bond is instrumental in acquiring affect regulation of the neurophysiological and psychological circuits or systems, which go from being carried out by another, a caregiver, on the outside, to being internalized by the child who gradually becomes independent and autonomous in affect regulation.

Parents and caregivers have a special role in fostering and facilitating the proper growth and maturation of systems that lead to appropriate development. And yet sometimes they become the vehicle of and the source of vulnerability to future trauma and even of dissociation and psychopathology (with insecure or disorganized attachment) for several reasons, as listed below:

1. Because of their own insecurity of attachment and a residual trauma of human agency, mostly from maltreatment but also from violence of any

kind (so that they cannot protect their own child from fear and anxiety and might in fact provoke those reactions in the child).

2. Because they cannot protect their children from an external threat, because of their own incapacity to function as an emotionally secure base for their children (mostly because they did not have a secure attachment themselves with their own parents), or because of personal stressors (divorce, death of a loved one, unemployment and subsequent economic problems, illness and so on).

3. Because, in order to release their own frustration and rage at having been abused as children, they continue the cycle, performing violence on the helpless, simply because they are easy targets.

4. Finally, because they have dissociated areas in their mind and personalities that they may transfer unwittingly on to their children, as a result of their own dissociated areas in mind and personality, of traumatic origin. The connection happens through the subcortical areas of the right hemisphere, as illustrated by the interdisciplinary research of Allan Schore, who has described the links between development,

attachment and neuroscience in both normal health and psychopathology and to whose extensive interdisciplinary research I recommend the reader to refer (see Schore, 1994, 2001a, 2001b, 2002, 2003a, 2003b, 2010, 2012, 2016, 2016, 2017, 2019a, 2019b).

Mechanisms of transmission of trauma (through attachment and psychodynamics) in first and second levels of traumatizations

An attachment bond is instrumental to the acquisition of affect regulation of the neurophysiological and psychological circuits or systems, so that the regulation initially provided by a caring other in the external environment, usually a maternal adult, is finally internalized until the young being is independent and autonomous. Affect dysregulation, impulsivity and destructiveness will create life-long difficulty in experiencing a sense of trust, self-esteem and hope, when facing future traumatic situations, therefore they disrupt the neurobiological capacity for a resilient response.

In humans and in other mammals, positive experiences in attachment have long-term effects on the hypothalamic–pituitary–adrenal axis (HPA), with the immediate release of noradrenalin which plays a decisive role for the regulation of biological synchronicity between one organism and the other and in the child (Bradshaw and Schore, 2007; Schore, 1994), connecting right brain to right brain of the two beings (Mucci, 2021).

These transactions take place with the greatest intensity in the period of maximum increase and development of the right brain (the first 18 months of life for the human infant). The caregiver's function is therefore fundamental for the development of the individual; the mother (or whoever takes care of the child) functions as the regulator of socio-emotional development during the first years of the child. This subtle emotional regulation influences or permanently alters the levels of activity of the brain and plays an essential role in the formation of the limbic system[2] (Ziabreva et al., 2003, p. 5334), fundamental for emotion, memory, an empathic response, and therefore for future emotional life and cognitive and social functioning. Proper care and response in special maturational moments are critical towards optimal development.

Other studies confirm that the attachment relationships have a strong impact on the limbic and cortical areas of the right hemisphere (see Cozolino, 2002; Henry, 1993;

[2] The limbic system seems to be the site of developmental changes associated with the rise of attachment behaviour, particularly of the right hemisphere which is in a growth spurt in the first two years of life (Anders and Zeanach, 1984; Joseph, 1996; Tucker, 1992; Schore, 1994).

Schore, 1994; Siegel, 1999; Tweedy, 2021), influencing images of self, other, and perception of one's body in relation to the external world (regulated mostly by connections through the right insula in the limbic system). Limbic areas, which are subcortical, mediate affectivity and the cortical areas have a regulatory and control function over impulses. In borderline patients, this connection and good regulation between limbic areas such as the amygdala and cortical areas are lost or impaired, explaining the affect dysregulation, originated by the early misattunement with the caregiver or even abuse.

In the interactions between the child and the caregiver, the latter is a source of experiences that shape the genetic potential of the child, acting as a psychobiological regulator of hormones that directly influence the genetic transcription. The mother or the primary caregiver is the environment of the child, as the hidden regulator for the child, starting from day one, from gestation. Through these mechanisms, psycho-neuro-endocrine processes that take place during these early critical periods are responsible for a permanent impact on the genomic patrimony, which in turn influences the development of the brain circuits.

Attachment is common to all mammals, but in humans, besides the internalization of the affect regulation system (which is the basis for the capacity to fight stress, revert vulnerabilities and remain steady in the emotional response and centred in one's own identity, all contributing to what we simplify as the process of resilience) has the important consequence of making the mind capable of the achievement of that complex system that we have described as moral or humane behaviour enriched by socio-cultural/family/personal values, including the levels of our superior consciousness, self-reflective evaluation of behaviour, capacity to feel guilt and remorse for evil doing. Humans in fact achieve or construct an internal, abstract representation of the internalized feelings and emotions connected to the attachment figure, which Bowlby calls 'internal working models' (and we might call 'implicit working models') because they are implicit (based on the amygdala recording), internalized representations of the dynamics of attachment, affecting our view of ourself and of the other. That is why in borderline disorders the way the individual views self and other is always distorted and very biased (what Kernberg calls 'identity diffusion', even though he does not refer this internalization to the attachment system; and I add to this 'identity diffusion' the level of 'sexual identity diffusion' – see Mucci, 2018).

In humans, the limbic system (which ideally, in optimal upbringing, would be connected to the cortical areas, connecting emotions to control, planning and deferral of impulses) is the site of developmental changes associated with the rise of attachment behaviour, particularly of the right hemisphere, which is in a growth spurt in the first two years of life (Anders and Zeanach, 1984; Joseph, 1996; Schore, 1994; Tucker, 1992). This subcortical base, in connection with the orbitofrontal and prefrontal cortex, articulates the complex moral system and higher-order control and cognition, with impulse control, capacity to cope with frustration and planning of more adaptive behaviour. Besides emotion, clearly identified by Damasio (1999) as a basis towards our decision-making capacities and behaviour, the construction of meaning is the most important element for our capacity to choose, and this 'construction' requires the necessary hardware or matrix for the actual choice and behaviour.

Since the developmental structuring of the brain, connecting the amygdala and the entire limbic system with the higher orbitofrontal areas, is not innate but the result of actual maturation influenced by care from at least one caregiver, this explains the special role that parents and caregivers have in the growth and education of the young, together with our education systems. It is also so important, allowing for the proper growth and maturation of systems that lead to the highest and most appropriate human development, including responsibility and morality (in the neuroscientific sense of choosing between what is best in evolutionary terms) or altruism and empathic capacity.

Many of the failures of caregivers to respond to the needs of the child *derive from their defences* against the capacity to recognize or comprehend *in themselves* similar negative affects. For instance, in the case of a traumatized parent, the child's expression of pain and fear might provoke in the parent similar affective states and might conjure up unresolved issues, to the point of the parent's not being able to recognize the same affects in the child (Lyons-Ruth et al., 1999).

The mother's defences originate from her own developmental story and, in turn, might make it difficult for her to respond empathically to the affective states of the baby. These defensive responses reflect well-established characteriological models, whose presence can be inferred/deduced on the basis of the interviews undergone during pregnancy (Fonagy et al. 1992).

A parent in difficulty experiences the following issues:

- They are emotionally inaccessible, therefore not in tune with the emotions that the child expresses and not capable of reducing the levels of hyper-arousal and distress of the child.
- They might contribute, in fact, to high levels of arousals and stimulation, instead of working towards soothing those stressful states.
- They are not capable of repairing the hyper-stimulation of the interaction, leaving the child

in a state of distress for long periods of time (affecting all the regulations of the systems).

- Particularly when the child is distressed but in general in interactions, these caregivers are more insensitive, irritable, critical, punitive and show less warmth and flexibility or even cruelty and maltreatment in the interaction with their children, often with the perception of being maltreated by the child herself (as indicated by the protocol of strange situation with disorganized parents) (Ainsworth & Wittig, 1969).

The result of all this behaviour, if not repaired by another caregiver or early psychological intervention, is the creation of insecure and disorganized attachment (with the vulnerabilities to psychopathology we have discussed) and the style of attachment will be passed on to the new generation who will then, as parents, repeat the same cycle of suffering, abuse and lack of care.

In the case of a frightening or frightened parent, inducing disorganization, the child tries to defend themselves from this parental stress-creation in a way that affects the development of the child's nervous parasympathetic system and subsequent cognitive development. According to Kernberg (1975), this would explain the typical tendency of borderline patients towards dissociative defences ('splitting defences'), which result in dissociated states of the ego. Research also shows that the cognitive preconditions for dissociative defences are established between twelve and eighteen months of age (Gergely, 1992), which coincides with the period of maximum intensity for mother–child regulation and for brain development. In Schore's developmental model, if there is trauma (lack of attunement) in this period, there is the establishment of vulnerability towards borderline disorders (at twelve months) or narcissism (at eighteen months).

Figure 3.2 illustrates my understanding of Schore's phases of pathological traumatic development (from Mucci, 2018).

Notwithstanding the importance of the genetic components in the development of the brain, it is also essential to consider that many caregivers suffer from unresolved trauma, grief, depression, addiction or borderline personality disorders, so that the alteration of their mental state, chaotic and dysregulated, impresses itself on the developing brain of the child and on the Self in formation through the exchanges of the regulatory function between the right brain of the mother and the right brain of the infant. As Draijer and Langeland (1999) argue, following Schore, *this intersubjective psychopathogenic mechanism mediates the intergenerational transmission both of the relational trauma and of the dissociative defence intervening against dysregulated and overwhelming affects.*

Attachment

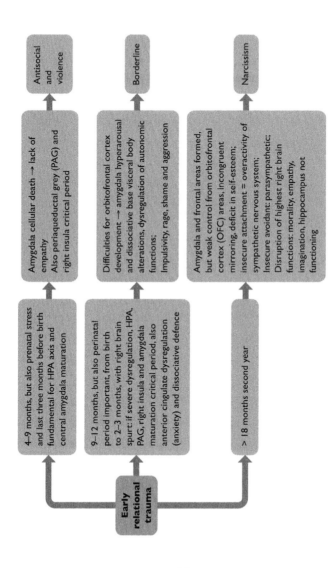

Figure 3.2 *Developmental etiological moments of traumatization in the first two years of life. Redrawn from Mucci, 2018*

Relational traumatic experiences are stored in the imagistic procedural memory of the visuo-spatial right hemisphere, the locus of implicit and autobiographical memory (Hugdahl, 1995; Markowitsch et al., 2000; Schiffer et al., 1995; Schore, 2010). Unresolved trauma in the caregiver causes alterations in the emotions and in the management of stress and of the regulatory function in the relationship with the child, alterations and disturbances that, in turn, have an impact on the regulatory functions of the brain of the developing child.

In line with this model, research demonstrates that severe dysfunctions in psychiatric patients are associated with serious maternal dysfunction (Draijer and Langeland, 1999) and that physical abuse and extreme adverse conditions in care giving are associated with dissociative somatoform disorders (Roelofs et al., 2002).

Regarding other factors that might influence the relationship negatively, Bowlby has specifically indicated that alcoholism, depression and marital conflict are factors that predispose forms of rejection of the offspring and could lead to abandonment and severe neglect (Bowlby, 1969, 1973). Surprisingly, he has never explicitly referred to physical violence and sexual violence (on the part of the parent), but obviously abuse can be added to the list.

Silent dissociation: even in lack of abusive behaviour as a result of trauma and dissociation in the parent

Through the right-brain connection between the two minds in the process of child-care, the creation of dissociative states in the offspring can be the outcome of growing up with dissociated parents, even when they do not mistreat or abuse the child. They are the silent mechanisms of dissociation. When caregivers enter (implicitly, unconsciously) those dissociative states, it is not possible for them to provide the affect regulation necessary to the young to promote optimal growth, with the acquisition of self-regulation of all the systems, and help them construct a positive image of themselves. I take the processes of the internalization of the 'alien self' from Peter Fonagy but suggest that this is not caused simply by lack of mirroring but by aggressiveness and harm towards the child. Following this concept, I argue that, in the case of severe abuse, a negative image with neural correlates of dysregulation is created in the child, affecting the 'internal working model' (IWM), and all subsequent perceptions of self and other, disrupting future relationships and social perceptions and behaviours.

To summarise, secure attachment has been described as the basis for future health, both physically and psychologically, and functions as a protection for both trauma of natural cause or of human agency, whereas disorganized attachment, carrying with it dissociation, together with hyperarousal, is the basis of future severe psychopathology (if not repaired in time). This needs to be intended in the sense that, when we find suffering, destructiveness and psychopathology in an adolescent or an adult, we need to look at their developmental years and possibly at the aetiopathogenesis in those first years of life to understand the path between vulnerability and (precarious) resilience that has led to psychopathology. Other caring relationships might have intervened in the meantime, creating more resilience and better adaptation and a less dysfunctional outcome.

Behind very resilient stories, in addition to the potential protection towards vulnerabilities, there is the capacity of restoration built in by further caring attachment relationships, especially in years in which neurobiological development and maturation are still possible. The brain is very plastic for longer than we might imagine, certainly into adulthood, with neocortical development taking place until the age of 20–25 and plasticity lasting throughout maturity (Gross, 2000). Neurogenesis has been seen in the hippocampus throughout the life span (Eriksson et al., 1998). Following the developmental story of some individuals, we might sometimes be surprised by the actual strength and beneficial adaptation they show. Determinism is always a poor means of understanding psychopathology: we need to look backwards for an understanding of the aetiopathogenesis only when we have psychopathology in the adult (which does not mean that we should not do whatever is possible to avoid or repair trauma, neglect and stressful conditions as soon as possible). In the case of developed and diagnosed psychopathology, we unmistakably find that there has been a problem in upbringing and/or in the family, even starting in previous generations. Signs of improvement and restoration as the child grows up are already a sign of resilience, stemming from both biological reasons and environmental circumstances throughout the life span. We have endless evidence of extremely successful outcomes resulting in the good integration of adult personality traits in ways that seem incredible when the events of the first years of life are considered. Neuroplasticity is a major factor attesting this resilience, but there also needs to be other environmental reasons for neuroplasticity beyond genetics, resulting in epigenetic changes, in order for repairing factors to be triggered. We can see this in early adoption under good circumstances: the earlier the child is adopted under good environmental circumstances, the better the result in growth and health.

Under appropriate conditions and the right expertise, therapy is certainly a motor for reparative neuroplasticity activation (with changes in gene expression that alter the strength of synaptic connections and interconnections in the brain, changing paths of conditioning, sensitization and extinction of responses) and we now have functional magnetic resonance imaging studies showing this (Kandel, 1999; Linden, 2006). Nevertheless, we need to be aware that vulnerabilities in individuals might leave them with a predisposition to cumulatively affect their personality and their behaviour. In this case, future exposure of the subject to subsequent trauma, at different ages and in consideration of future life cycle difficulties or future stressors, might impede or impair the capacity to be fully resilient and be restored to health and stability because of this cumulative effect. And we should not forget that attachment dynamics (secure, insecure or disorganized) are reactivated by future love or meaningful relationships and by future exposure to trauma. Having a new child is one of these mechanisms of reactivation of attachment dynamics in the parent (reactivating not only neurobiology and emotions rekindled by IWMs of child and parent but patterns of imagery, imagination and expectations about the newborn, and continuity of one's own life through the new generation).

Dynamics and consequences of traumatic attachments (first and second level of trauma of human cause)

In order to evaluate the security of attachment, Mary

Ainsworth developed the protocol of the 'strange situation' in which secure attachment (B) correlates with maternal sensitivity, whereas children (group A) who had less sensitive, indifferent or hostile mothers, would react by avoiding interaction, or would reproach the mothers, or look away from them, or show ambivalent behaviour, looking for contact and at the same time refusing it (C), whereas the so-called group D, insecure–disorganized, presented contradictory freezing states, with stereotypies and anomalous gestures in relation to abusive parents, who induced fear in their children, often in the presence of a 'frightening/frightened parent' (see also Lyons-Ruth et al., 1987). A frightened parent, possibly because of their own trauma, might frighten the child because the latter is in the paradoxical situation of being put in a stressful situation by the very person who should reassure them. The situation is made worse if, when faced with a danger, the parent shows the desire to avoid being near or in the presence of the child. In recordings, parents of group D showed subtly threatening behaviours, invading the personal space of the child, following him or her, using unexpected or slightly threatening gestures.

We should note that children whose parents were abusive were found to be disorganised in 80 per cent of cases compared with 20–40 per cent of the control group (Carlson et al., 1989). The profoundly negative effect of early relational trauma (i.e. early abuse and severe neglect in the very first years of life), generating a disorganized/disoriented pattern, will not only act as a risk factor for possible psychiatric disorders (Schore, 2001, 2002, 2003b), but also, unless remedied by reparatory events, persist into adolescence and adult life. It will contribute to the establishment of repeated patterns of the same behaviour in different relationships, affecting future attachment relationships, for instance, in future relationships with a partner, with one's own children and, also, affecting the therapeutic relationship.

Most importantly, the disorganized attachment bond will mediate the traumatic effect even in future traumatizations, so that disorganized children will react to future traumata – even accidents or catastrophes that are not man-made, with no human relations implied – with less resilience and more psychological damage (depression, personality disorders, addiction or other problems). In cases of future trauma of human agency, the traumatic reaction will be compounded, leading to weaker resilient outcomes. This happened to Israeli soldiers fighting the Six Day War: the worst affected were second-generation children of Shoah survivors (see Solomon et al., 1988; see also Laub, 2005b).

Dissociation[3] as a consequence of disorganized attachment

Giovanni Liotti, the Italian evolutionist–developmental clinician and researcher, in a study aimed at verifying the hypothesis that children with disorganized attachment are more prone to develop dissociative disorders (Liotti, 1992a; Liotti et al., 1991), asked patients with dissociative disorders if their caregivers had lost a significant other in the first two years of their lives. The hypothesis was confirmed. Loss and death of a significant other for a parent are among the major causes of stress that might create difficulties in the care of the child. According to Liotti (2004), disorganized attachment due to maltreatment and abuse caused by caregivers may lead to dissociated images of the self, resulting in a metacognitive deficit that induces dysregulation of emotions (in accordance with Kernberg's model and Schore's findings) and incoherent and unintegrated multiple representations of self and other (which create 'identity diffusion', in Kernberg's language), which activate both the attachment system in the child and a defensive system, so that the integrative functions of consciousness

---

[3] Dissociation describes a process of disconnecting from one's own thoughts, feelings, memories or sense of identity. The dissociative disorders that require professional treatment include dissociative amnesia, dissociative fugue, depersonalization, derealization and dissociative identity disorders.

are hampered, resulting in split images and moments of dissociation.

Disorganized attachment and vulnerability to dissociative behaviour (the basis for most severe pathology) and sometimes repetition of violence

A non-traumatized caregiver – a parent with no drug or alcohol problems, who is not addicted to the internet, is not depressed, does not have any mental problems or other severe disturbances that can impede good care giving, and who remains accessible to the child even after momentary separation – is in the best position to respond appropriately to the emotional demands of their baby and elicit all the positive exchanges of affection through moments of attunement, play, harmony and well-being, facilitating growth, health and a future resilient, fulfilling and joyous adaptation to the circumstances of life.

On the contrary, a caregiver with difficulties cannot keep the attunement with the child required for optimal regulation and cannot provide the continual re-attunement required for 'interactive repair', after common moments of rupture. In a secure and sensitive caregiver, the attunement is automatic, non-verbal, and visuo-facial, rooted in right-brain and bodily communication.

When the fundamental tuning in the first 18 months

of life between the child's right hemisphere in formation and the right hemisphere of the mother does not take place or, more accurately, if the rupture is not repaired regularly, there is what Schore describes as 'early relational trauma' (Schore, 1994, 2003a, 2003b, 2016). This I consider the first level of trauma, which results in higher levels of stress – with higher cortisol levels and higher glucocorticoids, impacting the HPA axis system, contributing to a state of hyperarousal of all the systems and possible dissociation in the long run, including a reduced immune response. Not only is the child left alone in the regulation of his or her states, and the homeostasis of all vital parameters (remember the rat pups in the epigenetics studies by Meaney, 2001 and Hofer, 1994 becoming immediately dysregulated in their vital systems namely heartbeat, body temperature, sleep and eating when the mother is absent and does not nurture and lick them), but the formation of the self, meaning the awareness of one's states, needs and self-esteem, is not well established. The self is born from the other, out of this constant development of awareness of one's own bodily and mental states in construction, thanks to the presence of another who acts in response to the child's states. This dual (co-constructed) regulatory function builds the basis for the correct appreciation of stimuli both from outside (exteroceptive) and inside (interoceptive) the body. There is the growing perception of one's own bodily needs, in connection to a growing, gradually forming image of the self. One's image of self could be of one that is easily soothed, sensitively cared for, loved and 'important' for the environment or of one that is despised, annoying, problematic or even exploited by the environment for its own needs, an undesired being whose very existence is difficult or rejected. These relationally built and implicit working models construct the image of internalized Self and Other. Starting with the very first relational exchanges, the working models are constructed through the body of the child in interaction with the body of another. The child's Other could be a biological mother, a father, an adoptive parent or whoever is involved in the necessary care that the newborn requires. We carry with us the mental and physical traces of this other, who was caring or uncaring towards us in our upbringing.

Even though it might sound obvious, poverty, poor diet and even pollution, besides other stressful conditions, all contribute to stress for the newborn or even the fetus. Allan Schore has devoted a long study on the effect of toxic conditions, physically and mentally, on the development of newborns, and the research showed that, mainly due to hormonal interferences, the male fetus and male child is the most fragile and most affected organism under difficult situations (Schore, 2017).

Schore underlines how secure attachment depends on the

mother's psychobiological attunement, not only with the infant's cognition or behaviour, but rather with the infant's dynamic alterations of autonomic arousal (i.e. the energetic dimension of the child's affective state). For this interpersonal communication to succeed, the caregiver needs to be psycho-biologically attuned to the dynamic crescendos and decrescendos of the infant's bodily based internal state of peripheral autonomic nervous system (ANS) arousal and central nervous system (CNS) arousal. Therefore, 'through right-brain-to-right-brain, non-verbal visual–facial, tactile–gestural, and auditory–prosodic communications, the caregiver and infant each learn the rhythmic structure of the other and modify their behaviour to that structure, thereby co-creating a moment-to-moment specially fitted interaction' (Schore, 2001b, p. 203).

A wealth of research shows the consequences of parental stress on children (Perry et al., 1995; Schore, 1994; van Ijzendoorn et al., 2011), including the adverse childhood experience research mentioned in Chapter 1, illustrating how trauma in childhood and being raised in a dysfunctional family affect the immune system and the various body systems that might be influenced (cardiovascular, metabolic and so on) and psychomental health.

Several studies have shown a link across frightening maternal behaviour, dissociation, and disorganized infant attachment (Liotti, 2004; Lyons-Ruth, 2003; Lyons-Ruth and

Jakobvitz, 1999; van Ijzendoorn et al., 1999). When the caregiver enters a dissociative state, expressed through freezing states (with eyes unmoving and half-lidded and 'altered' tone, with simultaneous voicing and devoicing), the child enters a fear alarm state (Hesse and Main, 2006).

Neurobiology and psychodynamics of *second level* of trauma: abuse, maltreatment, incest create insecure or disorganized trauma

Various studies conducted on high-risk families have associated maltreatment with disorganized behaviour (De Bellis, 2001; George and Main, 1979; Lyons-Ruth et al., 1990). As discussed, in the study conducted by Carlson and colleagues (1989), 82 per cent of maltreated children were disorganized; in other studies (Cicchetti et al., 2006) the results were as high as 90 per cent. The maltreatment was perpetrated by depressed or addicted mothers. Months later (at 22 or 33 months), Kochanska (2001) demonstrated that children with disorganized behaviour presented higher levels of aggressiveness and rage compared with those of dismissing, resistant, or insecure children.

The combination of disorganized or preoccupied attachment with ongoing abuse and relational violence in the family constitutes the major risk factor for bodily and psychological pathologies. In the results of work by Paris and

Zweig-Frank (1997, 2001), patients with or without abuse had an elevated score on the dissociative experiences scale (DES), meaning that there is dissociation with or without abuse. (We have already clarified how a parent can cause dissociation in the child even when there is no abuse, because of the communication of the dissociative dynamics and contents through the right brain of the caregiver.) Interestingly, the correlation of a high DES score and compulsive behaviours such as eating disorders (not anorexia but rather bulimia and over-eating) and drug and alcohol abuse has been studied and proved (see Mucci, 2018).

Incest, especially between father and daughter, or mother and daughter or son, is considered pathogenic to an extensive degree. It breaks trust and brings violence where it is most unexpected, within the family and from the caregiver, and confuses all subsequent parameters between what is good and bad, beneficial and destructive, what is right and wrong, what is a matter of power and what kind of obedience is owed to an adult, disrupting the construction of the very symbolic order (which the Oedipus prohibition in fact helps construct, if we want to think in terms of Freudian theory, even metaphorically). Interestingly, Ilse Grubrich-Simitis explains the lack of distinction between reality and fantasy in these survivors as the outcome of the traumatic breach of the incest barrier

(Grubrich-Simitis, 1981). Since the blurring of the border between reality and fantasy is a psychotic breach, we can understand how dangerous for the human psyche incestual and incestuous transgressions are (this difference between incestual and incestuous is in Racamier (Racamier, 2010) and I have used this distinction in an interesting case of complex PTSD in *Borderline Bodies*, in the case of Dorothy, Mucci 2018). All major life issues and identity formations are a matter of separation and proper confines: incest deletes and blurs the very possibility for children or adolescents to come to know themselves and to establish an order and a safe boundary between self, other and the outside world (Rachman and Mucci, 2022).

Intergenerational dynamics of transmission of trauma of second level (maltreatment abuse incest)

As we have seen from excerpts from Sandor Ferenczi's *Clinical Diary* (1932a), the pressure that the child experiences when forced, in order to survive emotionally, to agree to a vision of reality that is not true, as in a family with unrecognized abuse and incest, in order to avoid further violence and pressure, makes them dissociate from that part of the conscience that contains unacceptable or incompatible views, which will remain encysted and alienated from the Self (see also Abraham and Torok, 1994). These are precisely the elements that are likely to be transferred intergenerationally in future relations (even through silence, as split parts of the self through right-brain communication mechanisms) and we should remember that the bond with the child rekindles the system of attachment (with one's own parents and caregivers, for better or worse). Philip Bromberg has aptly illustrated this incompatible view within consciousness as the dissociated parts that have to be disavowed: 'dissociation narrows one's range of perception as to set up non-conflictual categories of self-experience' (Bromberg, 2011, p. 43).

The painful experience received from the environment, and mostly from somebody who should take care of the child (the mother, the father) leaves a permanent mark in the personality, creating 'a split in the personality', a change in the child's behaviour. This is Ferenczi (as early as 1932a, from his *Clinical Diary*):

'From the moment when bitter experience teaches us to lose faith in the benevolence of the environment, a permanent split in the personality occurs … Actual trauma is experienced by children in situations where no immediate remedy is provided and where adaptation, that is, a change in their own

behaviour, is forced on them – the first step
towards establishing the differentiation between
inner and outer world, subject and object.
*From then on, neither subjective nor objective
experience alone will be perceived as an integral
emotional unit ...'*

(Ferenczi, 1932a, p. 69, author's emphasis)

This blurring of boundaries leads to the transferral of unconscious content and meaning between parent and child,
and is also the cause for the cognitive distortion we already
explained; it is very evident in personality disorders with
fragile reality testing. It also implies that the child experiences
the guilt of the incorporated aggressor, a point illustrated by
Ferenczi (see the *Clinical Diary*), besides the introjection of
the aggressiveness of the molester, which becomes turned
against the self or against another (1932a, p. 190).

The passage above clarifies how the distortion of truth
calls for a change in personality because the child feels the
necessity to adapt to that distorted reality (the reality of what
the perpetrator says is true), what for instance, Jay Frankel
has recently called 'compliance with the aggressor' (2011),
discussing in detail the consequences of this behaviour not
only for the subject but for society at large.

Attachment

More than in massive social trauma, this kind of personality disorder with distortion of truth and blurring of
boundaries between inside and outside, between me and
other, is a typical after-effect of abuse, both psychological
and physical or sexual, in distorted long-term relationships
and what we have termed complex PTSD, including incest.
As Ruth Leys has written, commenting on Ferenczi's passage,
'more fundamental than any other traumatogenic factor',
including the actual sexual assault to which Ferenczi gave
rightly so much weight: '[…] was the lie and the hypocrisy
of adults that, forcing the child to doubt her own judgement
about the reality of her experience, fragmented and hysteri-
cized her' (2000, p. 153); and, I would add, condemned her
to silence and compliance.

Simply put, what the child is deprived of is their own
truth in connection with her experience of an event that is,
at its core, relational and the implication of this is that the
distortion is going to be repeated, without the child being
aware of it, in future relationships including the analytic one.
As Lewis Kirshner writes, 'trauma impairs the child's capacity
to evaluate reality, a tendency which may subsequently be
re-enacted in psychoanalytic treatment where the patient may
conform to his/her analyst's authoritarian interpretations'
(1994, p. 221). And, he further explains: 'Unless the analyst
actively establishes a different kind of relationship with her

patient in which acceptance and equality are manifested, she has little chance of helping the analysand discover the historical truth of his traumatized past' (1994, pp. 221–2).

This kind of hypocrisy was the target of Ferenczi's criticism of Freud. The dissociative dynamics that, at an individual level, impede the recognition of truth, at societal level are transformed into denials and primary process regressions to primordial dynamics of defence, against fear and helplessness and impotence, with envy, oblivion, aggressiveness and splitting or indifference, and denial of facts (as in negationist processes of the Holocaust and other genocides) and social numbing or indifference, which are very widespread nowadays but difficult to understand unless we also consider wider complex society psychological dynamics (see also Harris, Kalb and Klebanoff, 2017a, 2017b).

Attachment, abuse, neglect and creation of antisocial disorders

In their work on attachment, reflective functioning and borderline disorders, Fonagy and Target have underlined how attachment relationships are causal in inducing or inhibiting the development of the self-regulatory systems of the brain (Fonagy and Target, 2002). Secure attachment will affect the reflective capacity with regard to one's state of mind and those of others, therefore the capacity to mentalize, a fundamental construct identifying a capacity that is scarce (a deficit) in so many pathologies, in particular personality disorders; what by definition borderline patients cannot do is mentalize, i.e. putting themselves in the mind of the other (Fonagy et al., 2004).

Moreover, it is likely (Liotti, 2005) that a faulty functioning of the process of cognitive monitoring or 'mentalization' (Fonagy et al., 2003), or a deficit in the capacity to reflect on experience, is probably an obstacle to the elaboration of the memories of traumatic events and therefore facilitates the development of PTSD, dissociative disorders and borderline disorders. Therefore, in this way insecure attachment becomes another source of future traumatization. Other studies demonstrate how a deficit of reflective functioning and of the capacity for mentalization (which should normally derive from a good attachment system) is also responsible for a deficit in the capacity to develop empathy (Baron-Cohen, 2011; de Zulueta, 2006), with extreme consequences for the individual and society, since a low degree of empathy could result in cruelty, serious disinhibition and criminality.

We know from other sources (Kernberg, 1992) that anti-social behaviour represents the extreme end of borderline personality disorder. This means that, when something 'goes wrong' in the attachment process (to use de Zulueta's expression), the entire limbic system, the regulatory system and the connection between the limbic system and the orbitofrontal system are affected and impaired. In this way, the development of empathy (and mentalization) is affected so that violence and emotional dysregulation and impulsivity may result, meaning more sources for traumatizations for the population (these people may become responsible for criminal acts, violence, on themselves and others, and abuse).

In Allan Schore's model, antisocial development is linked to very early traumatization, often in prenatal phases, or afterwards, between the age of four and nine months, causing cellular death and reduction of the amygdala, which will be difficult to repair, and permanently impairs the capacity to feel, connect emotionally and socially, and experience empathy for the other. It is also linked to having suffered severe deprivation from a very early stage. We should distinguish nevertheless a kind of antisocial behaviour that shows callousness, insensibility and ruthless behaviour in a sort of cold attitude, really dis-human, as in some serial killers who kill in a cold way, and the kind of criminal acts that derive from lack of control of very destructive impulses and aggressiveness. In both cases, of course, the connection between areas linked to emotions and the higher-order areas of control and tuned-in empathy is totally disrupted.

In the antisocial and psychopathic personality (in a

continuum of severity from minor to maximum), a number of biochemical abnormalities have been indicated (e.g. serotonin, monoamine oxidase and hormone dysfunctions). Again, there might be different views as to how much of this disruption is genetic, but we have seen how the early environment, which can contribute positively or negatively to all phases of development, is the maternal prenatal nurturing and subsequent stages of care. It might therefore be influenced by epigenetic disruption, through mechanisms called methylation of DNA, capable of altering permanently and through time the expression of genetic transcription or determining the silencing of certain genes. Children with conduct disorders, with or without attention deficit hyperactivity disorder, are considered to have an elevated risk for antisocial and psychopathic personality disorders in adolescence and adulthood (with or without comorbid disorders, such as schizophrenia and substance abuse). And, as already indicated, there are substantial gender differences, with a much higher number of men manifesting this behaviour than women and a higher rate in women for spontaneous remission or improvement in behaviour (see, for a review, Martens, 2000).

Take the case described by Alessandra Lemma in her book *Under the Skin* (Lemma, 2010), of a young man who ended up in a forensic hospital, having killed his mother by throwing her down the stairs during a fight. He had received all kinds of abuse, physical and emotional, including having been sold sexually by his own prostitute mother who was also a drug addict. We can easily imagine that the mother might also have been the victim of abuse and exploitation in her life, as well as possibly being diagnosed with antisocial behaviour and a possible personality disorder.

Attachment and transmission of trauma of the third level (genocide)

THIRD LEVEL OF TRAUMA: MASSIVE TRAUMATIZATIONS AND HOW THEY ARE CARRIED THROUGH GENERATIONS BY WAY OF ATTACHMENT

Trauma of the third level (massive social traumatizations as in war or genocide as in the Holocaust) in the first generation might result in mental, psychological and physical pathology, as studied in numerous articles and essays on this topic, even though no general agreement or scientific findings exist, except in clinical practice. The very idea that survivors might be 'marked' by physical ailments and emotional disabilities is repugnant to those survivors who have indeed come out of the experience with amazing resilience and exceptional well-being. Nevertheless it is common knowledge that the people who actually survived the war, the camps and internment did suffer traumatizations that impacted on their physical and psychological health, with long-term consequences and even intergenerational transmission. So, to speak of a 'survival syndrome' (as several clinicians and theoreticians have done, themselves often survivors of the camps) might no longer be culturally and personally acceptable. Nevertheless, I would like to first take a look at what William Niederland, one of the first clinicians studying survivorship and a survivor himself, wrote in 1981, and then to highlight what the cultural trend of the research has been more recently.

The major characteristics of the syndrome in the first generation of massive trauma of this kind were:

1   *Chronic or recurrent episodes of depression; with neurological and rheumatic pain, backache, gastrointestinal disorders and muscle weakness (therefore, depression and somatizations of various kinds).*

2   *Anhedonia, in connection with the unelaborated loss, resulting in depression and a permanent state of sadness and grief; with the incapacity to feel and search for pleasure, even in aspects of one's everyday life and social life.*

3   *Anxiety, linked to the constant threat that persecution might come again (as in Primo Levi's recurrent nightmares that he was still in the concentration camp).*

4   *Hypermnesia, meaning constant remembering and flashbacks of traumatic circumstances (the opposite of amnesia or dissociation).*

5   *An altered sense of self and identity, influencing body image and self-image, in connection with alterations in the perception of time and space, perceived as having been damaged forever within the self.*

6   *Clear psychosomatic conditions such as peptic ulcers, cardiovascular disease, hyperthyroidism, asthma, hypertension [...] insomnia, headaches, gastrointestinal disease.*

(Niederland, 1981, pp. 414–19)

The fact that some survivors might not have developed those symptoms obviously depends on a wide variety of reasons. The first hypothesis, besides mere chance or luck, and less severe exposure to atrocities, was the presence of a security of attachment as a mediating neurobiological force that made them face extremely stressful conditions with a different capacity of emotional and effective control, with better adaptation and more refined skills, enabling them to find solution and emotional support, often with the help of other inmates, and thanks to the presence of relatives and children, keeping a sense of hope and an inner core of certainty that eventually they would be saved (and would defy the Nazi regime in order to describe the atrocities to the external world, as is reported by several survivors). An organism already accustomed to high levels of stress and destructivity would lack (under renewed and sustained stress) the lucidity, the control and emotional strength and the power to sustain itself and find better ways out. This lucidity is probably one of the reasons that made some people decide to leave their hometown at the first signs of a shift in political attitudes towards Jewish people, with the first racial laws being implemented as the Nazis started to acquire power, whereas others stayed. Also, another relevant element of resilience was the actual capacity to support each other and sustain one another, both among relatives and friends, as described in the memoirs of Primo Levi (1996), Elie Wiesel (2006), Anna Ornstein (2004) and many others. Memories of attachment bond were very clear in the interviews I viewed at the Fortunoff Archives.

Among the pre-existing non-biological factors that lead to better resilience in the survivors, besides security of attachment and favourable conditions, I would include:

1. The possibility (or the capacity, also partly due to secure attachment) of remaining together, maintaining hope, supporting each other, and the capacity to keep an intimate and sound connection in the midst of total annihilation, physical, mental, psychological (for example, in the case of Elie Wiesel with his father).
2. The capacity and possibility of maintaining rituals of community, as testified by several survivors who kept their prayer recitals and other communal rituals alive, as Wiesel attests with the description of the sense of inner psychic survival and endurance through the recital of morning prayers with his father.

All forms of mutual support and constant bonding might become sources of resilience and, in turn, must have been made possible by secure attachment, in a continual cycle of good reinforcement, because excess cortisol, the major stress hormone, can be reduced by touch, love, physical closeness and emotional connectedness, creating positive feelings, including those triggered by religious faith and spirituality. All of this would have created a sense of safety, protection, community, belonging, and hope that would have enhanced a more careful and more controlled behaviour and making parents more capable of protecting their offspring. Oxytocin, a neurotransmitter and hormone that neurobiologically characterizes all bonds of attachment, makes parents fight for their children, while reducing their own level of stress. At the same time, it is likely that it was the very security of attachment (meaning, the internal capacity to keep a memory or implicit bond with attachment figures, usually parents, or lovers or husbands and wives) that made it possible for them to maintain their own bonds of love, with faith in the possibility of a favourable outcome, maintaining utmost vigilance against threats and perils and even against levels of destructiveness in themselves and protecting them from feeling utter depression and desperation.

As Wiesel wrote in his memoirs *All Rivers Run to the Sea* (1995): 'Those who retreated to a universe limited to their own bodies had less chance of getting out alive, while to live with and for a brother, a friend, an ideal helped you hold out longer.' When his father died, Wiesel sank into a state similar to that of the Muselmann described by Levi, a body with a dead spirit inside: 'For all practical purposes, I had become one of the "Muselmann" [sic] drifting beyond life, into death and into water, no longer hungry, thirsty, or sleepy. Fearing neither death nor beating … I did not line up for bread or soup, I waited for nothing and no one. I drifted through time and sank into a dreamless sleep. When I woke up, I didn't know where I was' (Wiesel, 1995, p. 95).

In addition, in the camps a source of emotional vitality was kept alive through remembering and connection to attachment objects (both people and objects that served as reminders of loved ones) or memories: a mother's apron, the smell of broth, the words of encouragement and moral direction given by a father, and so on. Attachment memories constituted the only 'familiar' home and base and reference in this place of utter devastation and erasure of meaning. Having lost that connection, if deprived of memories of attachment, 'one is not at home in the world anymore' (Langer, 1989, p. 35). As Wiesel evocatively writes: 'It is because I remembered that I could remain human' (Wiesel and Heffner, 2001, p. 148).

Visiting the Fortunoff Archives for Holocaust Video Testimonies at Yale University, and viewing just a few of the tapes (from the nearly 4,000 kept there), what was really striking were the elements of connectedness, community, attachment and bonding the survivors shared in the camps and described in their interviews. It seemed that doing something for another, a child, a cousin, a mother, a friend, or maintaining a meaningful human contact, was a great source of strength and hope, clearly fostering positive emotions, which certainly contributed to their resilience and capacity to survive. A survivor I interviewed, who was actually born in the camps, admitted that what really kept him alive was probably (possibly even more than the love of his own mother) the presence and constant support and love of all the women of the community, especially the unmarried women who considered him a gift of love and hope from God in those bleak days.

In the tapes, it was mostly memories of everyday rituals (sitting at the table for meals, images of ordinary routine such as the women cooking, the smell of the meals at the Shabbat table and so on) that created a web of connections, in which body, experience, memory and reconnection kept the survivors grounded in the difficulties of the present and in the determination to survive.

ATTACHMENT AND MOURNING IN MASSIVE TRAUMATIZATIONS

Sagi-Schwartz et al., (2008) have shown how, in accordance with Bowlby on the elaboration of mourning in children, the proper handling and intermediation of adults in the acceptance of loss is fundamental to proper mourning. Children need a honest and undramatic communication of the death and, at the same time, the support and tenderness of the caregiver, since the process of mourning means not only adaptation to external changes but an entire subtle readaptation of their inner world to internal representations and attachments. This cannot be done by the child alone (see Bowlby, 1969; Sagi-Schwartz et al., 2003, p. 398.)

We can imagine how many children, orphaned not only by the Holocaust but by other genocides and wars, right up to the present day, have been unable to properly mourn their loss, and are left with feelings of sadness, impotence, helplessness, rage and even guilt. Guilt is a highly likely emotion after the death of a loved one through lack of proper elaboration, at all ages. In Italy, every other day a woman is killed by a male relative, and often children are the witnesses. The outcome of this peculiar form of 'genocide', known as 'femicide' ('*femminicidio*') is still to be calculated.

As Freud explains in what remains a masterpiece on loss and mourning, 'Mourning and melancholia' (1917/1953), guilt is the common legacy of unelaborated rage at having being abandoned without reason, so that, as Christopher Bollas (1987) explains, 'the shadow of the other' falls onto the subject, with the internalization of negative and hostile feelings that become 'melancholia', or major depression, as we would say nowadays. The conditions in which trauma (in this case, loss) is experienced will be determinant in constructing forms of resilience, as the presence of insecure attachment with the lost parent or loved one will intervene negatively in the process.

Very often this kind of support was not possible for children who survived the Holocaust and children who survived other massive devastating circumstances. Often these children lost their parents without even being aware of how they died, nor did they have a place to properly mourn them, to express their grief and give some closure to their loss. That is why the physical presence of a gravestone or tomb, or a place to pray and remember and keep a connection with the dead, is fundamental in providing some solace to the pain, with some restitution in meaning and some closure for the event. Also, to remain without a significant attachment relationship afterwards makes resolution of trauma almost impossible. In this case, therapy might offer substantial help towards healing, even though to look for help once you have no other internal attachment pull is very difficult; the actual request for help might be triggered only by the utmost desperation, even without any expectation of relief. Patterns of avoidance of relationships or, on the contrary, dependence, in the surviving children's personalities have been observed (Hoffman and Shrira, 2019).

Another famous study (Sagi-Schwartz et al., 2008), using the adult attachment interview (AAI), found that 42 per cent of 48 subjects who had lost both parents in the Holocaust presented with very high levels of 'U' (unresolved trauma for loss) and clear signs that mourning had not been elaborated.

In the AAI protocol, this is clearly indicated by simple signs such as using the present tense for a loss that took place over a year ago. In this study, the conclusion seemed to be that the children did not have insecure or disorganised attachment, while the parents still suffered from the effects of the Holocaust (Sagi-Schwartz et al., 2003), which suggests that the parents had a secure attachment with their own figures of attachment (which might even have contributed to their survival) and did not transmit their unresolved trauma to their children.

Two correlated studies conducted by Sagi (2002) with non-clinical samples in Israel, including Holocaust survivors and a control group without a Holocaust background, have evaluated the lack of loss elaboration through AAI and other tests. The findings have shown that even after fifty years, children who had survived the Holocaust presented with the final score of 'U', and signs of unresolved trauma and mourning. The authors also underlined that loss, *per se*, was not the major reason for the presence of unelaborated mourning and that this condition was complicated by a state of disorganization which interfered with the mourning process. These studies confirmed that survivors of the Holocaust presented a much higher rate of disorganization in comparison to the control group (Sagi 2002).

RESEARCH ON THE TRANSMISSION OF MASSIVE SOCIAL TRAUMATIZATIONS ACROSS SECOND AND THIRD GENERATIONS

In a ground-breaking study in 1998, Yehuda et al. suggested that children of Holocaust survivors constituted a high-risk group for PTSD, since they presented with a greater prevalence of lifetime PTSD compared with a control group with similar exposure to traumatic events, as described in DSM-IV. The group of children of survivors also presented with a greater prevalence of mood and anxiety disorders. In another study, Yehuda et al. (1998) found that, in a sample of Holocaust survivors and their adult children in which PTSD could be evaluated directly, lifetime PTSD was present in the children of parents who either had never developed PTSD or had recovered from it. In a 2000 study, Yehuda and colleagues found that parental PTSD appeared to be associated with unusually low cortisol levels in their children, even in the absence of lifetime PTSD in their offspring (Yehuda et al., 2000). It is therefore likely that low cortisol may constitute a vulnerability marker related to parental PTSD, as well as a state-related characteristic associated with acute or chronic PTSD symptoms.

A study undertaken in 1988 by Solomon et al. found

that those soldiers who were the second generation of the Holocaust exhibited a higher rate of combat reactions two to three years after the war, compared with those without a Holocaust background. In addition, the Holocaust group recovered more slowly from combat reaction in comparison with the other group. Inter-generational transmission of this type of post-traumatic stress reaction (i.e. combat reaction) was attributed to secondary traumatization (Rosenheck and Nathan, 1985). The Solomon et al. study (1988) is especially important because it presents some systematic evidence for transmission effects across two generations, but despite these interesting results, most studies did not present large differences between the second generation and control subjects with regard to psychopathology.

In her article 'Transgenerational transmission of effects of the Holocaust', Irit Felsen (1998) presents an overview of the clinical studies, empirical studies and unpublished doctoral dissertations on the title topic up until the late 1990s, since the appearance of the first article by Rakoff et al. (1966). Felsen's article presents a discrepancy between the clinical studies, in which the hypothesis of transmission seems tenable, and the empirical studies, which have rendered a much less consistent view, due sometimes to lack of control groups or a reliance on anecdotal data or other biases. The empirical studies seem to show that, as a group, the offspring of Holocaust survivors do not demonstrate psychopathology, in contrast with what clinical studies testify. However, many findings point to measurable differences between the research group and the control group, with reduced feelings of autonomy and independence, and heightened anxiety, guilt and depressive traits, with difficulties also in the regulation of aggression (Felsen, 1998, p. 57). It has been suggested that the differences are not unique to survivor families but to Jewish families in general, so that they are cultural rather than specific to the survivor group. It is suggested then that, in future, research comparison groups should include children of eastern European Jewish immigrants. In addition, it seems desirable that the characteristics observed in the offspring group should not be considered as reflecting a psychopathology but should be contextualized within a theoretical model of personality development including psychoanalytic object relations, cognitive developmental psychology and attachment theory and research; gender differences should also be considered.

In another important overview, Zahava Solomon et al. (1988) present a retrospective of the literature, concluding on one side that Holocaust survivors are a high-risk population with special intrapsychic characteristics, including anxiety, depression, guilt, anhedonia, emptiness, despair, somatization and oppressive preoccupation with traumatic memories (Danieli, 1981; Eitinger, 1961; Niederland, 1968), but overall the various studies 'show members of the second generation to be an essentially healthy and functioning population despite certain difficulties that apparently derive from their parents' Holocaust experience' (Solomon et al., 1988, p. 79). Though the second generation in Israel is not prone to psychopathology more than the rest of the population, it does suffer from peculiar intrapsychic difficulties, especially under certain particularly stressful circumstances.

In a more recent qualitative study on 'Intergenerational transmission of trauma across three generations' by Rachel Lev-Wiesel at the University of Haifa (2007), a preliminary investigation on this transmission was carried out across three generations, across three types of trauma experienced by the first generation. The first trauma included experiencing the Holocaust, a second was being placed in a transit camp following immigration from Morocco and the third was being forced to dislocate as a result of war. Members of subsequent generations were interviewed regarding their life as survivors or victims, or as the second or third generation of survivors/victims. The content analysis showed the intergenerational transmission of three types of trauma across the generations.

More recently there has been a shift from focusing only on the disfunction and maladaptation of survivors to high-lighting their resilience and strength (Barel et al., 2010). The findings vary widely and once again they seem insufficient

(Bar-On et al., 1998). The same discrepancy of views exists in the transmission of trauma to the children, who were found at risk in several studies (Felsen, 1998; Yehuda et al., 1998), especially under extreme stress conditions (Barel et al., 2010; Solomon et al., 1988).

Meta-analytic results suggest that intergenerational transmission of Holocaust trauma to subsequent generations is observed, in particular, in studies with clinical samples (Barocas and Barocas, 1980), as in studies with weaker design based on convenience samples (Sagi-Schwartz et al., 2008; van Ijzendoorn et al., 2003).

Research by Amit Shrira and his group at Bar-Ilan University has evaluated the intergenerational effects on physical health on second-generation adult children, finding hypertension due to high cholesterol, higher blood sugar and obesity (Shmotkin et al., 2011). They conclude that the functioning of the three generations shows general resilience along with specific vulnerabilities, interwoven within family dynamics as, for example, parent and child gender, time of birth, number of children in the family, number of survivor parents (it makes a difference if both parents were survivors or only one, and if the mother was the survivor, since, as Yehuda has shown in research we will analyse later, epigenetic transmission is more on the maternal side than the paternal), parenthood relationships, Holocaust-related communication and exposure to stress. Finally, expression of stress might remain latent in adult children unless they are exposed to further traumatic situations.

According to Shrira, models to read the data take into consideration different factors:

- early relationships (shaping mostly self-perception, identity and personality);
- models of socialization (they are raised to be suspicious, diffident, afraid of others), therefore with a negative world view, with cognition rooted around threats, in the emotional domain, in anxiety, guilt, negative feelings;
- patterns of communication (parents have been too emotional in their narration with them or on the contrary have avoided any reference to their experience, maintaining silence on certain issues as a family secret);
- bodily dysregulation of affect (dysregulation of adrenalin and cortisol in particular).

In my opinion, all of these variables can be present and need to be taken into consideration when we try to evaluate and understand the impact of trauma on subsequent generations and these children's responses in terms of vulnerability, because of a cumulative effect or resilience. All these variables interconnect and can intervene in complex and somehow unpredictable ways (at least in the sense that before a thorough exploration we might not know all of the intervening factors). Moreover, as we have repeatedly argued, several elements might be unknown, dissociated, disavowed or truly forgotten, and to rely on the memory of the subject might be difficult so that to recover the historical truth and concatenation of events might be a painstaking activity.

Nevertheless these variables are useful in determining levels of functionality as well as understanding diagnosis. During treatment, they should guide the understanding of the difficulties experienced and the areas to focus on for better restitution and healing. To these features I would add the specific dynamic patterns that several psychoanalysts have identified in their clinical work with first, second and third generations (as shown by Laub, Kogan and other experts; see the specific sections on psychodynamic therapy and on these unconscious dynamics).

A review study conducted by Barel et al. (2010) analysed the emotional difficulties of survivors, and they found higher levels of existential anguish, anxiety and emotional discomfort compared with the control group. Also, Scharf and Mayseless (2011) in a study on 'Disorganizing experiences in second and third generation Holocaust survivors' found that second-generation Holocaust survivors might not show direct symptoms of post-traumatic stress disorder or attachment disorganization, but are at risk at developing high levels of psychological distress. Based on in-depth interviews with 196 second-generation parents and their adolescent children, the study identified three themes of disorganizing experiences across generations: focus on survival issues, lack of emotional resources, and coercion to please the parents and satisfy their needs. In turn, the assumption was that these themes reflected the frustration of three basic needs: competence, relatedness and autonomy; the frustration becomes disorganizing because they threaten a basic stability, potency, confronting the individuals with incomprehensibility and helplessness. The research also pointed at the detrimental effects of trauma on people emotionally close to the victims, for example, spouses and children (see Maloney, 1988), therapists of trauma victims (McCann and Pearlman, 1990), and Israeli war veterans (Hobfoll and London, 1986; Solomon et al., 1992).

On a cautionary note, Rachel Yehuda and Amy Lehrner point out in the evidence of epigenetic changes and transmission of trauma to further generations, 'the most compelling work to date on the topic has been done in animal models, where the opportunity for controlled designs enables clear interpretations of transmissible effects. The scarcity of human studies due to the methodological challenges they imply, it is uncertain that we can attribute intergenerational effects in humans to a single set of biological or other causes. Our biology is too packed with multiple perspectives, individual, cultural, societal, to really allow us to arrive at one definite response' (p. 243).

Nevertheless, a previous study directed by Yehuda and her team at Mount Sinai Hospital School of Medicine, in collaboration with Michael Meany at McGill University, Canada, on the 'influences of maternal and paternal PTSD on epigenetic regulation of the glucocorticoid receptor gene in Holocaust survivor offspring' found mechanisms of intergenerational transmission of trauma-related vulnerabilities especially linked to the maternal side (Yehuda et al., 2014). The study has shown that the presence of PTSD in mothers is responsible for the effects and the change in methylation (one of the modes of epigenetic change), whereas in the absence of maternal PTSD, offspring of paternal PTSD do not present the same findings. In particular, among offspring of Holocaust survivors, maternal PTSD was associated with increased risk for developing PTSD, whereas paternal PTSD was associated with greater risk for major depressive disorder.

PSYCHOANALYTIC AND PSYCHODYNAMIC
CLINICAL WORK WITH SURVIVORS

In spite of the research on groups, mostly showing areas of greater resilience than expected given the highly traumatic and desperate circumstances, psychoanalytic clinical work on individual cases of second- and third-generation survivors, as described by Robert Jay Lifton, Judith Kesternberg, Dori Laub, Henry Kristal and other survivors and clinicians, does show the difficulties of the parents in child-rearing. This traumatic upbringing, sometimes in presence of sick, emotionally unavailable parents, constantly anxious and afraid of going back to previous traumatic conditions, deeply influenced the upbringing and the internal dynamics and therefore the personality formation of the children intergenerationally.

The parents' difficulties, as highlighted elsewhere, might not only be due to the war or the genocide conditions. Severe loss, trauma and abuse do have intergenerational consequences, as I have shown in clinical studies with children of traumatized/traumatizing parents (Mucci, 2018). It actually seems, reading all the research on the first, second and third levels, that the worst consequences are due to the presence of disorganization of attachment already in the parents or, in any case, the cumulation of levels of trauma and their presence in the parents seem to predict major destructive consequences. In other words, as the study of Sagi-Schwartz and his group (2003) on grandmothers who still suffered psychological consequences while the children did not show serious pathology, it would seem that, to rephrase the data in psychoanalytic terms, the internal good object of the grandmothers might have created a shield for the next generations.

Alexithymia and somatizations: traces of massive traumatizations in the body

The first generation of survivors often suffers from severe somatizations and severe alexithymia, a difficulty in feeling and naming emotions in mind and body. Following Henry Krystal, himself a survivor, we can see traumatic somatizations as a way of expressing through the body the excessive emotional impact, impossible to elaborate, and of triggering a mechanism of 'regression of affect' (Krystal's definition, Krystal, 1968).

We should distinguish between alexithymia and somatizations due to extreme affect regression and massive traumatization, as in the first generations who survived the Holocaust, and alexythimia in the second and third generation of survivors who did not experience the extreme trauma of the genocide but might have had a parent who was depressed, alexithymic and prone to severe somatizations, in place of the expression of the unspeakable traumatizations (see also Mucci, 2018 on psychosomatic developments as an intergenerational deficit). Therefore we need to distinguish between somatization of an intergenerational nature (because of the lack of protection in the developmental phases, as seen in many young adults today) and somatizations as severe regressions in the systems of those who have experienced the massive traumatization that Krystal has described as extreme collective traumatizations, such as the Holocaust, with extreme affect regression (called also 'decathexis', in psychoanalytic terms, prevalence of death-drive and loss of libido), or, in French psychoanalyst Andrè Green's terms, 'de-objectalisation' (Green, 1993), destruction of the internal good object. In psychoanalysis, an internal good object is the formation of a symbolic, internalized state of safety and trust in self and other. Rephrasing this concept in attachment language, it is the sense of safety and security given by a 'secure base' or secure attachment, which stems only from good primary relationships with a caregiver (not necessarily a biological one, but any person equipped with enough sensitivity for the long process of bringing up the child).

Somatizations in second and third generations of survivors seem to be associated with lack of parental emotional protection, due to the very disconnection with one's own body and feelings, therefore the presence of insecure attachment *in the parents.* Psychoanalytically, this has been explained by Krystal with regression of emotions of traumatic origin and by Joyce McDougall as the presence of a 'symbiotic bond' between mother and child, in which the mother does not protect the child (McDougall, 1989).

In *Borderline Bodies* (Mucci, 2018), I have described how in the very absence of maternal protection if the mother has been too sick or absent (as in the model by André Green of the 'dead mother complex', a metaphor to express the actual lack of protection and emotional contact between a depressed, sick or psychically absent mother and the child), somatizations might stem from this difficulty in the establishment of the representational shield that works as a protection in mediating between the perceptions received in the body and the emotional and hormonal responses of the subject.

The body of the mother intervenes subconsciously and through non-verbal emotional connections and touch in establishing this emotional pattern of connection between body and mind (between the two bodies and the two minds). When there is disconnection and lack of attunement between the two, the higher symbolic shields of representation and secure objects cannot be formed in the mind of the child, making the proper elaboration of negative emotions impossible so that they remain disavowed or evacuated through acting out and addictions. Alexithymia is, in a sense, the creation of this lack of an emotional shield between mind and body: I can't feel, I can't express, I can't verbalize to myself or another what I feel, therefore I speak through the body and I let my body express (to the point of organ damage) the unrecognised pain that eventually affects tissues and organs; this mechanism in which emotions are not read by the mind and/or verbalized, might activate other automatic responses in the body–mind system to evacuate the unbearable and unfelt emotions, as in eating disorders (with the exemption of anorexia), alcohol and drug abuse.

Alexithymia, the incapacity to feel and be connected within and to the body, represents one of the most severe responses to long-term exposure to traumatizations and to overwhelming, unelaborated emotions. Unacknowledged emotions nevertheless unconsciously guide and influence behaviour, together with denied and dissociated parts that are therefore projected; the growing disconnections between emotions, body and appreciation of emotions in the self is a severe problem in adults and in younger generations. These fragmented selves and emotional disconnections are all signs of intergenerational transmission and disconnection and they lead to acting out, heavy drinking, eating disorders and other destructive behaviours (self-harming of various kinds) as ways to counteract the lack of feelings or the inability to verbalize and mentalize what they are going through.

Laub and Auerhahn: 'reverberations of genocide' on to following generations

Laub and Auerhahn see an 'unconscious organizing principle for future generations' (1984, p. 153) in the way traumatized people view reality and the relationship they are involved in. The generations following the traumatic events construct inner psychic representations that are reflective of this external massive trauma: 'The more profound the outer silence, the more pervasive was the inner impact of the events' (p. 154). The imagery of the Shoah seems to be present as a cultural trait even in non-Jewish patients. Among the themes that the two authors often find present in therapy, are:

- fear of loss of bodily integrity (what traditionally could be considered castration themes, meaning that the Oedipal phase is problematic);
- super-ego pathology: extremely harsh super-ego instances, together with extremely strong urges and desires in addition to super-ego lacunae, such that rules and values cannot be taken too seriously if the very issue is survival;
- unstable or feeble object relationships, fear of loss, separation and disruption;
- nurturing of others and identification with victims, and/or fantasies of rescuing others;
- the external world is experienced as precarious

and unstable, full of violence and corruption,
so that lack of trust, alienation and duplicity are
common in relationships;

- fluidity of boundaries between self and other,
past and present, reality and fantasy;

- a view of the parental generation as damaged, vic-
timised, unable to protect themselves; and also a
sense of helplessness and doom about themselves,
that nothing can protect the subject from possible
future disasters and genocides; so that a status of
hypervigilance and distrust is always present; extreme self-assertiveness as a way to defy enemies;

- problems in the ego ideal and object representation, stemming from narcissistic omnipotent
imagery;

- inhibition of fantasy, especially incapacity to fan-
tasize about pleasure and excitement (Ibid).

It is striking how some of these features highlighted by
Laub and Auerhahn conjure up the traits of what we would
define as a borderline structure today, with identity diffusion, primitive defences, unstable relationships, emotional
turmoil and difficulties in attachment relationships, mood
disorders, and reality testing still retained but feeble and
somehow distorted.

In another seminal article, 'The primal scene of atrocity' (1998), Auerhahn and Laub testify to how the experience of unheard-of atrocities has contributed to a rewriting of unconscious structures and fantasies, such as the so-called primal scene as described by Freud (1918, the case of the Wolf Man.) In this case, the child came face to face with parental intercourse when entering the parents' room (without permission), with the potentially traumatic reaction due to overstimulation and lack of release and therefore anxiety, all of this creating envy and desire for revenge, as predicted in the Oedipal complex. What happens, the two authors ask, when extreme traumatization leaves no trace, such that no psychic representation of events is there, because they are outside the possibility of recording since 'massive psychic trauma lacks the associative network that characterises normative memories'? An example of this is when a survivor apparently cannot remember even having had a child who was killed by Nazis. And yet, this is their point: 'the trauma that can neither be fully told nor fully remembered by the first generation shapes the psychic world of the second generation' (Auerhahn and Laub, 1998, p. 361).

Their understanding of this problem, from having worked with and discussed several cases, is that:

> 'when metaphor is actualised, that is, when
> psychotic levels of experience are enacted, language

*and communication disappear; experience
becomes subordinated to images and a mothering
other is truly absent. This is especially the case
with those individuals tortured as children. Such
individuals have no internal positive representation
to which to return for restoration and healing and
hence are the most difficult cases to treat … Thus
what is … concretised in torture and massive
psychic trauma is the destruction, by aggression,
of the maternal introject. It is this destruction
that is beyond representation. The actual trauma,
being thus unrepresentable, disrupts the capacity
of fantasing per se … [I]t is this trauma, or
disruption, that survivors cannot articulate to
their children. Children of survivors are exposed
instead to parental stories and construct their own
Holocaust representations. But the children are
exposed not just to what is said – to the split of
state in which the feeling of nothingness is retained.
The children are exposed, in ways they also cannot
articulate, to the absence that is covered over by
parental myths (cf. Bollas, 1987). Beyond the story
that is told, children sense the actual trauma that
has yet to be made into a narrative.'*

(Auerhahn and Laub, 1998, pp. 363–4)

The authors observe that, just as the primal scene and Oedipal myth are stories of origins, children of survivors have the task of clarifying to themselves where the parents have been, where the missing children and relatives are, and which place has been reserved for them as a consequence of all that loss and destruction. Since 'what cannot be named or mourned is often identified with … therefore not only in every survivor but in many children of survivors is represented an internalised other who failed' (Auerhahn and Laub, p. 373). The authors conclude that 'without a mothering other, there is no universe, no God, and no life' (p. 375).

(5)

Therapy with survivors of human agency: to heal and redeem intergenerational trauma

1 THERAPY AS A PRACTICE OF CONNECTEDNESS AND TESTIMONY (RE-ESTABLISHING AN EMPATHIC DYAD INSIDE AND WITH THE OTHER)

The strength of the bond with the other is what protects the subject from inner extinction: it is literally what makes psychic life possible, starting from the neurobiological growth of the embryo, then of the human being, making possible the development of the brain and all biological, psychic and social life. In Ang Lee's 2012 film *Life of Pi* based on Yann Martel's 2001 novel, survivorship after a shipwreck on a raft is represented as the constant fight with a tiger on the same raft. But the relationship with the tiger, though perilous, actually gives the protagonist the strength and resilience to fight for life, to the point that the final moment of separation from the tiger is a concrete loss, though a liberation at the same time and a real new beginning. As we have seen, even a life-threatening relationship is better than no relationship at all for the life of the psyche.

The actual relationship with the other, a caring and committed other, allows both growth and reparation. It is, as we have argued throughout this volume, a dual process, both psychologically, in a real dual unconscious development, and neurobiologically, as in the right-brain dual connection between caregiver and child since birth, as described by Allan Schore and his theory of right-brain-to-right-brain communication and development.

Development is not possible without this connecting other, as the protocol of the 'Still Face' (Tronick et al., 1978; Tronick, 2007) clearly shows, and without mirroring and affect regulation of the emotions of the newborn. When less than optimal regulation of the neurobiological systems is available, the best formation of the self and its biopsychosocial functions are impaired, with damage to affect regulations and mental development. Psychically and mentally, the aim for the growth of the subject and development is to reach affect regulation, mentalization and control of impulses of the limbic nature with final higher-order control through orbitofrontal connection, and development of symbolic processes, control of emotions, creativity, social and affect higher-order cognition, with moral capacity to choose and plan and make prosocial decisions.

André Green's construct of the 'dead mother complex' (1993) is a good example of how the lack of the maternal gaze (maternal, paternal or any gender, since the care provided by the caregiver is a right-brain function that has no gender or biological sex attached to it, in a concrete way), in other words the psychic absence of a depressed or sick mother, creates a phantasm, a ghost, in the child, who then has to cope with the feelings or the devastation of that loss, with the feeling of inhabiting an empty space, an absence and a loss, which might become dangerous for the survival of psychic life.

Through the caregiver's care and proper sensitive emotional attunement, this bond allows the possibility of life as neurobiologically defined. On the contrary, where relational trauma (trauma caused by another human being) restricts and impairs life and growth, the impact can be defined as the psychological death of the subject, or at least as seriously affecting the subject's well-being and health. Interpersonal trauma is most severe when it comes from the closest and potentially most important family member, namely an attachment figure in the family inflicting violence or incest. It is this human and humane bond, this connectedness, that makes us human, or, in the words of Dori Laub, interpersonal trauma can be defined as the rupture of the 'empathic dyad' between self and other, that should sustain life. So that violence that stems from another human (from abuse in the family to the trauma of torture, rape, war and genocide) leaves in the survivor the most severe traces, fragmenting the psyche through dissociative structures (the basis for the most severe psychopathology) (Mucci, 2021a), as Giovanni Liotti has theorized, showing the connection between disorganized attachment in the child and vulnerability towards future dissociation, something that natural catastrophes or accidents do not create (Liotti, 1995).

Re-establishing a human connection when the survivor feels alone and disconnected from everybody is the first step in the healing process. It allows the establishment of the testimonial process between self and other, but it needs a truly committed and ethically engaged other. The testimonial process, so well defined by Laub, cannot leave the other untouched:

> 'For the listener who enters the contract of the testimony, a journey fraught with dangers lies ahead ... Trauma ... leaves, indeed, no hiding place intact. As one comes to know the survivor, one really comes to know oneself ... The survival experience, or the Holocaust experience, is a very condensed version of most of what life is all about

*... The question of facing death; of facing time and
its passage; of the meaning and purpose of living;
of the limits of one's omnipotence; of losing the
ones that are close to us; the great question of our
ultimate aloneness; our otherness from any other;
our responsibility to and for our destiny; the
question of loving and its limits; of parents and
children; and so on.'*

(Laub, 1992, pp. 72-4)

Survivors do not know their own story completely (what Laub
and Auerhahn (1993) call 'knowing and not knowing massive
psychic trauma') because trauma defies representation and
narrative retelling. Excess stress and glucocorticoids impede
the encoding in the hippocampus and so survivors embody
their traumatic story in their symptoms and behaviours,
which establishes repetition 'in place of knowing'.

In fact, the paradox of trauma lies in these questions:
how does one offer testimony about an experience that has
no psychic representation? How does one convey a memory that cannot be registered (Auerhan and Laub, 1998, p.
360)? The presence of a committed other is essential, the
'companion' for the journey that nobody can experience
alone (because it could even be dangerous for the psyche,
as in certain forms of art in which contact with previous

trauma becomes a mortal and perilous encounter).

In fact, survivors, if they are not in complete denial or if they are now reluctant to speak, often after having tried to tell their own story to no avail for lack of a good listener, feel a pressure to testify, an urgency. But, more important, as Laub stresses: *'they need appropriate circumstances – a totally present listener who creates the holding space for them to do it.'* But once they find it, they really allow it to come. And it comes out with a force. They don't want to stop ... There is a force to have it happen.' (Caruth, 2014, p. 48, author's emphasis).

Therapy with the tuned-in and ethically committed therapist creates this holding space, the channel for remembering and retelling one's own story and the collective story, which was missing. Regarding the ethical commitment of the therapist, I refer the reader to Judith Herman, who is very clear on this subject, against those clinicians who think that the issue of recovering truth is not our aim and hide their responsibility behind the veil of neutrality: *'The moral stance of the therapist is of enormous importance ... It is not enough to be neutral or non-judgemental. It is necessary to affirm a position of moral solidarity with the survivor'* (Herman, 1992, p. 178).

The reconstruction of the truth of the survivor needs the active presence and affective participation of others for survivors to restore their own truth and a place of internal safety where it is possible to remember and piece together these unconceivable or unbelievable truths. It is not something they can complete alone, and the social or collective scenery can be an element of further integration of meaning of one's experience.

To go through the perilous journey of testimony, the survivor needs the body and the mind and the care of another, trained to do this with the appropriate attention and attunement. The quality of this presence is of utmost importance and somehow, though training is fundamental, cannot be totally taught because it does not rely only on techniques and instructions. As for matters of responsibility and morality, they are linked to an individual developmental level, something closer to a spiritual position in the sense of a human quality, a dedication to the other that goes almost beyond one's own self. This kind of empathic surrendering cannot be taught, though it can be the fruit of several life experiences including first and foremost one's own therapy (for the future professional), together with the legacy of meaningful encounters with supervisors, colleagues and other significant human experiences. It pertains in my mind to a realm of lay sacredness that goes beyond personal interest and rational calculation and allows openness to the experience of thirdness, as the encounter and appreciation or acceptance with another within oneself, to meet a place of thirdness inside (Benjamin, 2004; 2018). I think a good way to understand this place of thirdness that is necessary to be the witness of the other's truth is described by Elie Wiesel in response to the question 'Am I my brother's keeper?'

> 'It is a question that Cain asked of God, having killed Abel: "Am I my brother's keeper?" And the answer, of course, is, we are all our brothers' keepers. Why? Either we see in each other brothers, or we live [we are doomed to live, I would say] in a world of strangers [therefore in an in-human world].'

(Wiesel and Heffner, 2001, p. 3, author's brackets)

And Wiesel adds:

> 'A century ago, by the time the news of a war reached another place, the war was over. Now people die and the pictures of their dying are offered to you and to me while we are having dinner. Since I know, how can I not transform that knowledge in responsibility?' (p. 3)

'So the key word is "responsibility". That means I must keep my brother.' (p. 4)

To my mind, 'I must keep my brother' means I must bear witness to the other's pain and their suffering, to their life journey within the realm of therapy and within the boundaries of the time and space we allot ourselves, both the patient and the therapist, in the treatment. I am their witness, or I am 'the witness to the truth of the other', a truth that the other might reconstruct or become accustomed to living with, thanks to the presence of a totally 'benevolent and helpful' other (Ferenczi's words, 1932a, p. 24), a companion in the journey of testimony, which does not spare anybody. It is thanks to the other, to another who is especially committed in their listening, that the survivor can retrieve the unacceptable pieces of their story, the story that was alien to themselves, due to dissociation, the parts that were split and erased, what constitutes the so-called 'unthought known' (Bollas, 1997), the unrepressed unconscious (Mancia, 2006), the traumatic 'knowing and not knowing'. This 'unthought known or this unrepressed unconscious' is not what has been repressed, but what we now understand as implicit memory, which expresses itself in enactment, in moments of dissociation, which are there for the sensitive other to pick up in the painstaking process of therapy with the survivor.

The internal addressee has been deleted by traumatization. For Laub, the traumatic fracture corresponds to or implies the lack or destruction of an internal good object which has been destroyed by the lack of empathy of the other, the aggressiveness of the persecutor, who has accomplished the deed, performed the harm.

This process of reparation is what I have called 'embodied witnessing' (Mucci, 2018) and this is why therapy with a survivor needs face-to-face contact of another; it involves all levels of mind, body, brain, in both participants and cannot be performed on a couch.

The pact of testimony is based on an internal/external 'connectedness' (Mucci, 2013), individually and collectively, which is at the root of what it means to be human – meaning that I belong to a community that shares similar values, primarily the preservation of human life as a sacred thing, and the fact that identity is based on bonding with all other humans, and therefore I fight to defend this sacred community at the root of existence. It is conducive to what Dori Laub calls 'creating a testimonial community' (Laub, 2005b). I strongly believe that we need to create and build a testimonial community concerning the destruction of human rights, which has become an urgent problem, not only for people slaughtered in countries unknown to us, but a testimonial community closer to home as well, to defend women from violence and murder in Italy, and women who are sold and killed elsewhere, to help adolescents alienated online and to defend those children who witness violence at home or are victims of it. We live in communities and cities that are more and more violent, more and more in-different, absent to ourselves, careless in our own process of increasing de-humanization.

For the survivor, the presence of the other, a certain form of presence, allows the reconstruction of this contact with the deepest self that is identified and can find its deepest self only in the wound, in the tortured body. Traumata would reveal themselves within the analytic journey 'provided the analyst is capable of housing them within himself/herself' (Borgogno, 2006).

That lack of an internal witness, i.e. the lack of an internal good object which constitutes the real traumatic damage and is responsible for the fact that reality is erased and therefore becomes split or dissociated, initiates the death drive and its destructiveness. Therefore aggressiveness is not innate, but stems from violence in relationships. To use Ferenczi's model, the victim has been identified with the destructive-ness and aggressiveness of the persecutor (1932a, 1932b), so that the persecutor's violence, aggressiveness and split guilt have been internalized by the survivor and re-enacted intergenerationally.

As Ferenczi wrote as early as 1932 in his *Clinical Diary*,

protesting against Freud that 'abreaction is not enough' and arguing that healing is the result of a real experience of connectedness and reparation of past wounds through an act of love: 'The catharsis gets bogged down, and how to remedy it,'

> *'It appears that patients cannot believe that an event really took place, or cannot fully believe it, if the analyst, as the sole witness of the events, persists in his cool, unemotional and, as patients are fond of stating, purely intellectual attitude, while the events are of a kind that must evoke, in anyone present, emotions of revulsion, anxiety, terror, vengeance, grief, and the urge to render immediate help ... "It cannot be true that all this is happening to me, or someone would come to my aid" – and the patient prefers to doubt his own judgement rather than believe in our coldness, our lack of intelligence, or in simpler terms, our stupidity and nastiness.'*

> (Ferenczi, 1932a, p. 24)

This witnessing capacity inherent in the truly 'benevolent and helpful' therapist, using the empathic capacity (what Ferenczi calls '*mitfühlen*', 1932a, p. 122), which nowadays abounds in all kinds of therapies, but which in those days nobody thought was a fundamental element in the healing process, is so simply but efficaciously described by Ferenczi in the following passage. He describes in such nuanced details how the traumatized body can be reawakened thanks to the attention, the sensitivity and the capacity of the other/analyst to really believe in the painful story that the patient brings to therapy. It is the emotional participation of the analyst that makes the body a sentient body and restores unity where there was fragmentation:

> '19 January: The analyst is able, for the first time, to link emotions with the above primal events and thus endow that event with the feeling of a real experience. Simultaneously the patient succeeds in gaining insight, far more penetrating than before, into the reality of these events that have been repeated so often on an intellectual level.'

(Ferenczi, 1932a, p. 14)

This is why, to use contemporary terms, mentalization (Bateman & Fonagy, 2004) or any cognitive acquisition of the events also would not be enough, if it remains a purely cognitive act. This is why interpretation by itself is not sufficient, or needs to come as the last version of a series of interpersonal reparatory experiences that go in the direction of the restoration of a meaning that was impossible to achieve without the integration of all the psychical parts. Also compassion and forgiveness cannot be taught or imposed (Mucci, 2013). The kind of connectedness and testimony we are calling forth here does not resemble the concept of thirdness as proposed by other clinicians, nor is it simply a 'feeling together', but it is a total and even bodily based disposition (starting from non-verbal aspects sustained by a complexity of neurobiological non-conscious disposition allowing that special connection of minds (Aron, 1996) or right brains (Schore, 2012, 2016), so that the unconscious of both participants in the therapeutic exchange is deeply involved, through implicit memory and communication through the right hemisphere, to achieve a real encounter of the experiences of the two people in relation, in practice of embodied witnessing in which mind body and brain participate fully (Mucci, 2018c).

It is the presence of the analyst, 'benevolent and helpful' and totally committed, acting as the interviewer in the practice of testimony who helps reconstitute the internal good object that has been destroyed by massive trauma and therefore (according to Ferenczi), emotions can be reconnected to 'the above primal events', therefore endowing that event with the feeling of a real experience. In other words, without that external witness who becomes an internal witness, the subject cannot retrieve the truth of their own experience, cannot believe it, needs to deny it, dissociate from it, so that from that moment onwards reality will be distorted. The survivor cannot believe the reality of their own experience, 'otherwise somebody would come to help' (Ferenczi, 1932a, p. 25).

Therefore, in order to achieve symbolization, I need an other who helps me reconstitute this essential trust in humanity that has been lost in traumatization.

In order for the other to arrive at actually voicing their truth, to express themselves through a retrieved capacity to speak, to symbolize, there needs to be a certain form of relationship, of contact, of connectedness. In fact, if the listener is not totally committed and available, the erased parts cannot be retrieved. For neuropsychologist Allan Schore, this kind of communication stems from the deepest recesses of the amygdala, within the limbic system (1994, 2001a, 2001b, 2002, 2003a, 2003b, 2010, 2012, 2016, 2017, 2019a) lateralized mostly in the right hemisphere.

With regard to the necessity of a committed and responsible other in order for truth to be reconquered, Laub almost echoes Ferenczi's words about the analyst as 'the only witness', the totally committed and empathic observer. In fact, Laub continues:

*'But to get it out in the interpersonal space there
has to be a companion. Basically I think it's also
the necessity for an internal companion, because
the process of symbolization and the formation
of narrative only happens within an internal
dialogue. And a listener temporarily takes the
place of that internal other, the addressee.'*

(Laub, 2014, in Caruth (Ed.) 2014, p. 48)

That internal other, found through the committed other, creates, in due course, an internal good object whose committed presence makes the putting of the pieces together possible, which allows the resilience itself, as Judit Mészáros has observed (Mézsáros, 2014). Laub also refers to this process 'connectedness', when he explains how for the testimony to come out, there already needs to be a certain level of ego structure: 'There has to be a certain amount of ego structure, a certain amount of object relationship, a certain connectedness, and appropriate others in order to speak' (in Caruth, 2014, p. 49). So, in order to restore some ego structure, some deep, dual interpersonal and intrapsychic work needs to have been done already, and this cannot come in the initial phases of treatment.

This ethical but also embodied interconnectedness is instrumental for healing to take place. Its functioning can be described neurobiologically (Mucci, 2018a) and its dynamics goes from embodied mirroring (a preliminary phase), to the actual working through of the emotions – of guilt, rage and desire for revenge.

Similar to Ferenczi on the vicarious traumatization for the abused child from the lack of support from the environment and from other potential attachment figures, Laub argues that: 'The loss of the internal other is often central to this collapse. You know that survivors often, to this day, have a disbelief of what they survived. "I can't believe I lived through that." And I see a version in myself as well' (in Caruth, 2014, p. 52).

This loss is the internalization of the complete death and destruction of object relations, if there were any to start with (if the survivor had secure attachment). This is, for Laub and Lee, the indication of internal devastation or annihilation, what they call the signs of 'erasure' and death drive derivatives, blurring the memories, and making representation as a secondary process impossible:

> 'The victim, to ward off the horrors of
> objectlessness, internalises and identifies with
> the only object available to him: the perpetrator,
> a bad object. Failure of the empathic connection
> and the consequent loss of the internal good
> object produce feelings of absence and of rupture,

a loss of representation, an inability to grasp
and remember trauma, and a loss of coherence.
Libidinal binding to associative links, to meaning
and to words, as well as to the internal object and
to oneself becomes at least temporarily suspended.'

(Laub and Lee, 2003, p. 441)

These death drive derivatives intensify the clinical manifestations of the consequences of massive traumatization. In our language, this internalization of the bad object explains, to follow Ferenczi's theory, the consequent identification with the persecutor, with guilt and shame on the side of the victim, and internalized violence on the side of the aggressor.

After the proper tuning in and appropriate mirroring as a way of using one's body (the therapist's right brain and empathic disposition and bodily disposition to help the patient), the next step in the treatment will be working through the negative emotions, of both the victim and the persecutor, guilt and shame on the side of the victim, and violence and aggressiveness on the internalised side of the aggressor

A dual path to renewed thirdness and testimony inside and outside

If trauma is the break of the empathic and humane alliance with the other (the 'similar to me' but also the 'different from me'), it is the inner and outer reconnection that has to be re-established through therapy, and it has to be reconnected both intrapsychically and interpersonally. It allows a space of thirdness and renewed possibility for one's own life to be regained (it is a rebirth, like forgiveness). I describe forgiveness as the interpersonal and intrapsychic work done in therapy that allows the actual elaboration and resolution of the victim–persecutor dyad, with the subsequent elaboration of the mourning process (Mucci, 2013).

Though connectedness and the symbolic ability to create some space of thirdness inside the self and the capacity to surrender are preliminary requisites for forgiveness to take place, forgiveness can result only after mourning and the working-through of anger, along with the surrendering of desire to take revenge and retaliate. Surrendering to the 'rhythm of the other' is fundamental to creating this thirdness, as in the example given by Steven Mitchell of his initial incapacity to 'surrender' to the pace and rhythm of his two-year-old child, following the child's timing and his pace as they were walking (Mitchell, 1988). Therapy requires the same capacity to tune in and be ready to intervene, without intervening necessarily and leaving the other the space to be and to remember.

No timetable should be embraced, no special timescale planned for emotional reconstruction, and yet an internal threshold of continual receptive alertness and presence is required. The linear, left-brain-constructed sense of timing will often be suspended because the timing of the trauma and the dissociative disconnections or memory block are not a linear process, but will be a cyclical time or recursive progression. No moment will be the same, at no moment will the patient and the therapist be in the same place mentally and emotionally, because the process of therapy changes them continuously. It is a not a simple process, nor an application of rules and techniques.

The vital and life moment is extraordinary and characterized by a constant flux of change, even though sometimes this consciousness will not be available even to the participants in the dialogue. (It is similar to a growing child – the changes will be impossible to observe daily by the actual caregiver but an outsider, who does not see the child regularly, will notice them very clearly and immediately.)

The first thing to learn is how to stay with the patient without imposing ourselves, our wish, our agenda, our timescale. It is part of what I define as mirroring, a process that has been defined as typical of the mother–child relationship, but I extend that process to not only mirroring of the internal states and emotions of the patient, but to the actual capacity to connect emotionally to the missing parts, the denied pieces of the story, the dissociated aspects, and to resonate with them, helping in their recollection. This kind of mirroring as the total acceptance of the experience of the other allows the process of affect regulation to flow and be repaired or re-established, and it is a dual communication through mind–body–brain (Mucci, 2018a).

While some traumatized patients need to learn how to down regulate the dysregulated affects, usually in hyperarousal (which they might do through bulimia, alcohol, drugs, self-harm), others (the more dissociated or alexythimiac patients, not in touch at all with their bodies and their emotions) need to learn how to read, feel, decode and embody their emotions. The therapist needs to work flexibly in both directions with different patients, as a very flexible and sympathetic instrument, down-regulating affects and dynamics in disorganized, impulsive patients, trying to make them aware and in touch with their emotions and to start recognizing the emotional connection between their acting outs (or enactments, if they happen in the session) and their emotions and bodily feelings.

The first step then will be to reconstruct the origin of the dysfunctional process, with the disavowed emotions, to be reconnected to their relational imprinting: self–other representations, implicit working models, victim–persecutor dyads with the two sides of affect, one associated with the victim side, and the other with the persecutor side, which have both become internalized and part of the enacted destructive behaviours, towards one's body and towards others (sometimes children or partner).

So when I say that the 'reconstruction of trauma' is the very first step in which both parts are involved, the patient and the therapist, we need to distinguish which level of trauma the patient has been victim of: lack of attunement and mirroring by the caregiver (level I) or also level II, with abuse, severe deprivation or incest? Or is the person a survivor of a huge traumatization, such as the immigrant fleeing from war and falling prey to more devastation, seclusion, violence, rape, torture and so on? Do they remember, or even over-remember their experiences? Or are they so disconnected that they live a sort of suspended life, with the actual traumata belonging to somebody else, being totally split in their personalities? There would be no point in trying to ask questions about the actual events until the survivor freely goes back to these events and emotions connected to them or has some re-experience and flashbacks of them. They need to be reconstructed through time as the relationship with the therapist becomes stronger, and it will be at the patient's pace, when more trust, confidence and a sense of security, safety and clear boundaries are achieved and kept. That sense of security allows the internal parts to be able to speak or come to the fore and be heard.

This happens usually in a phase that other therapies call the 'stabilization of symptoms', that is, creating a place of security and trust in the other, which is very often already a huge achievement. In fact, I cannot stress how fundamental it is with any patient, but with this sort of patient in particular, to keep proper boundaries and a reliable and steady commitment, all being qualities we communicate, even non-verbally, through our voice, our gaze, our steady and organized presence, keeping to a regular schedule, arriving on time, never missing a session or changing appointments as little as possible. Unpredictable behaviour on our part will resonate with the unpredictable and sometimes violent or brutal aspects of previous trauma, and with loss and regression. Stability is the first way of re-establishing a sense of order and care to somebody who has lost any sense of belonging to the human order. As with babies, and I say it without paternalism, rhythm and rituals are a fundamental way of organizing bodily and mental rhythms and re-establishing a sense of safety and perspective. As we go on with this constant care and attunement, the patient will unfold emotional aspects and events according to the representations of self and other images, following what we have called 'implicit working

171

models' (if we speak of trauma of first and second levels) or will have a framework to present the dissociated aspects. But, as Laub explains very well, those unrecognized parts need a true companion, a caring other and this is something that the mind and body of the patient can feel. I have described this way of being present and committed to receive the story and the missing parts of the patient as a kind of 'embodied witnessing', in which the mind–body–brain of the two need to stay in touch, through a right-brain (unconscious, or at least non-intentional and often unaware) connection in my previous work. It is a way of being connected that does not follow top-down pathways, meaning that they are not intentional, rational or planned, but they are bottom-up connections, meaning that they access bodily and visceral connections, including what Stephen Porges (2011) has called polyvagal connectedness. It means that the body receives connections through afferents from the environment, and the external body in front of me receives information through gaze, sound, facial expressions and bodily posture and disposition, and go from the nerves and sensories to the limbic system reading interoceptive and exteroceptive information, and connecting those sets of information to the deposit of implicit memories and present affects, positive or negative, and further elaborating through the superior orbitofrontal and frontal areas. The work goes from the body to the emotions to the mind and vice versa, and this goes from one person to the other, in a dual exchange, in a constant circuit of information and processing of emotions, going from the right brain of one to the right brain of the other, from the body of one to the body receptors and mind of the other, in a continual flux of constant communication and information, which at every step changes the very disposition of the body. Patients change rhythms and breathing, their heart rate changes, as do other parameters of neurophysiological regulation. And if we were to examine hormones and glucocorticoids and neurotrans-mitters, we would find changes in those neurobiological and electrical features too. All of this is accessed through verbal phrasing, putting into words what is felt at every step, as much as possible. The more the vessel that is the relationship becomes reliable and strong, the more it can hold, meaning that the mind of the patient becomes more permeable and stronger to be able to start reconnecting to pieces of truth that could not exist in that body and mind in that form before. As Bromberg very simply puts it: 'dissociation narrows one's range of perception so as to set up non-conflictual categories of self-experience' (Bromberg 2011, p. 43). Therapy, with the right timing and pace, allows this break-through and the reopening of those paths that had been narrowed in order to defend the subject from unacceptable truths or from exceedingly disturbing images and thoughts, and enables an integration that in turns makes identity stronger and healthier, capable of containing what seemed unbelievable or impossible to accept. Very often the traumatic moments were experienced by a subject who was too young or too alone to master the truth and the events, so one of the possibilities is that now, in the safety of treatment, the survivor can hold those truths from the perspective of an adult, or from the point of view of a stronger, not broken, subject.

So, the mirroring I am speaking about is actually the reconnection of two bodies and two minds, through the therapeutic encounter and pact. It requires also the actual participation in terms of empathy and even suffering, sometimes through the emotional and physical connections of the therapist's body. Very often I have felt in my body, through physical pain or nausea or other signs of emotional distress, what the patient was working through (and the patient would sometimes name it or describe it a moment afterwards) as if my body (and mind and right brain) could work as an intermediary towards the 'abreaction' of the feelings. And yet, as Ferenczi aptly writes, 'abreaction' is not enough, if it is not accompanied by the actual feeling of the corrective emotional experience, what Ferenczi often calls 'love' and what we can term the actual engagement of all the parts of the mind–body–brain of the therapist towards helping the patient, a double working-through. (I have further explained the mechanisms of mirroring in this sense of actually working through the missing parts and the disconnected emotions of the survivor in the case of Ariadna in *Borderline Bodies*, to the description of which I refer the reader (Mucci, 2018).)

The difficulty in this dual mirroring process of being completely capable of tuning in, attentive and available to the needs of the patient, is evident in certain mothers who are always in need of doing something but end up imposing their own views and needs on the child (often they end up being like the mothers of the schizoid personality type, intrusive and unavailable at the same time). The mother with secure attachment leaves a mental space in their mind for the child, even as she avoids imposing on and controlling the child. At the same time, the child needs to be 'alone in the presence of the mother', as Winnicott argues, meaning the mother needs to be emotionally present and receptive, even though she does not need to intervene all the time.

Intergenerational transmission, as stated repeatedly, will clarify the specific vulnerabilities inherited: for instance, the presence of an alcoholic mother, an abusive father, an incestuous brother and so on will all be elements to start with in the investigation. The patient will not know everything about their own story, but it will give you a route to stay focused and connected as the unfolding of the relationship with you continues. If a grandmother had been, for example, kidnapped, raped or even killed, not only the following generations will have the epigenetic legacy, as we have seen through research by Yehuda and others, but also you need to think what kind of everyday relationships, emotions, exchanges and care that the grandmother might have had with her children, one of whom is the mother of our patient, and keep in mind the deprivation, abuse, dysfunctional dynamics and attachments that have resulted from those old traumata. Although we said that we do not need to intervene or have an agenda in the reconstruction, we need to keep in mind the actual traumatic pieces of the story, as the patients moves through them, recognizing them, feeling derivatives of those traumatic attachments or denying them. Narcissistic patients (inheritors of humiliation and deprivation) will show a dismissive attitude or even a derogatory one towards their attachment, often idealizing their attachment figures in order to avoid the rage, wounds and humiliation experienced in childhood. But we need to keep in our mind the actual dynamics (the idealizations, deprivations, wounds) in order to understand the behaviour of the patient towards us, who is often not co-operative or even dismissive. At the same time, if the therapist were to name and describe the traumata undergone by the patient since the beginning, this would be of little use: the patient would not be able to acknowledge them. They need to be retrieved and often enacted in order to work on their emotional effects, now re-experienced in the treatment and the actual dynamics with the therapist.

In fact, the therapy needs to work and to reach the patient implicitly (through non-verbal and non-conscious interventions) and explicitly, verbally and consciously, going from the right hemisphere, the side more connected to the body and the unconscious, to the left, the more rational, secondary-process-based and conscious or deliberate side, with the aim of helping to re-establish the disturbed affect regulation, down regulating the emotions from the limbic system to the orbitofrontal areas. The patient might remember episodes from their past, as they deal with the here and now of therapy. As a result of this working at the 'regulatory edges' (Schore, 2012) of the window of affect tolerance, new connections between the patient's limbic–amygdala–emotional process and the orbitofrontal areas will be established, through the new positive relational experiences and the acceptance and the actual reassurance of the therapist, both verbal and non-verbal, ultimately and continuously allowing the integration and balance or regulation of the affects. What has been damaged in the previous relationship will have to be repaired through the new relationship. The process will move repeatedly from implicit and unconscious or dissociated areas to explicit and conscious and integrated areas, with the possible recovery of memory traces. During this process of recollection, intervening too early with interpretation will either be useless or even rejected if the timing is not right, if the actual opening towards acceptance of the truth of what really happened takes place but not at the right time, when the patient has already started the process of reconnection and re-elaboration. Interpretation given too early might in fact be felt as an invasion or a useless show of power and 'intelligence' of the therapist. As Laub and Auerhahn say: 'finally, because the traumatic state cannot be represented, it is unmodified by interpretation ...What is required initially in the therapy is not elucidation of psychic conflict but restructuring of the internal relationship between self and other' (Laub and Auerhahn, 1989, p. 391).

We should never forget how painful the entire process of reconnecting the emotional (and discarded) truth is, since it has created the split of personality and disavowal precisely to remain alive and survive.

This working through of the previous negative experiences will be relentless and repeated over months and sometimes years, and it is made possible by the constant re-writing of good positive relational experiences that will prevail over the negative past. The implicit working models will constantly be repeated, re-enacted and will cyclically disturb the progress of the treatment. Sometimes, the actual dredging up of buried memories might even trigger suicidal emotions, especially at the beginning. As the mind has to go through these threats from the past, the very birth of the hope that a new positive relationship might evoke with someone who, for the first time, seems available, caring and benevolent, might provoke anxiety and even the fear of having to be exposed to trauma again and be abandoned once more, left alone in the process. This might evoke the fear of further loss, abandonment and catastrophe in the patient, who might threaten suicide as a way to defend themselves from such exposure to renewed pain, loss and failure, so that even re-experiencing hope becomes a reason to be fearful.

But through time, if the process is guided by the emotional participation and an empathic relationship with the therapist, the two participants will experience the rebirth of hope and health, and the possibility of trusting oneself and the other. As the Boston Change Study Group writes:

> *'If the clinical process is affect-guided rather than cognition-guided, the therapeutic change is a process that leads to the emergence of new forms of relational organization. New experiences emerge but they are not created by the therapist for the benefit of the patient. Instead, they emerge somewhat unpredictably from the mutual searching of patient and therapist for new forms*

*of recognition, or new forms of fitting together of
initiatives in the interaction between them.'*

(Dell and O'Neill, 2009, p. 647)

This is consistent with what Liotti and Farina (2011) say about
what is actually reconstructed in the treatment, which is not
the repressed content of the experience, but the lived events
in their integrity, including of course the emotional, bodily
and concrete aspects of the experience. Poignantly they write:

*'It is worth stressing that the purpose of treating
traumatic memories is not to help the surfacing of
repressed content, rather, to reconstruct the lived
events in their integrity, to associate the different
fragmented components (emotional, sensorial,
motor, kinestetic), to assimilate them and to
enable their integration into the autobiographical
narration for the patient, in order to avoid or to
reduce their disorganising effect.'*

(Liotti and Farina, 2011, p. 191, my translation)

We are miles away from the Freudian concept of restoring
the Ego when there was the Id; it is not a matter of cleansing
the Huydensee of the unconscious and the repressed ocean

of drives and conflicts, but it is the actual reconstruction and restoration of the possibilities of development and thriving movement of life, had the traumatic events and dynamics not hit the patient so dramatically.

In this restorative process through a single life, a single patient, even future generations will be restored, because, as we have said repeatedly, trauma in one generation will impact on the very resources available to the parent for bringing up children and might create the distortions deriving from abuse and deprivation. So, to work through the trauma of one individual will be a way of redeeming a past that is epigenetically inherited therefore is at risk of being transmitted if the cycle is not stopped. What stops the cycle is the awareness of one's story, acceptance of one's past trauma, and this is possible through the reconnection that another enables and allows. It is a totally intrapsychic and interpersonal movement at the same time.

To break the cycle of victimization and violence, the survivor will have to confront the victim and persecutor identifications inside, with their emotions. To go through rage and the desire for retaliation is not only unavoidable but necessary, if survivors really want to get rid of the emotional ties that link them to the perpetrators and keep them in the psychological grips of the aggressor, even years or decades after the event.

This will mean that the reconstruction of truth cannot avoid a confrontation with the actual rage against the perpetrator(s), with what has very often been dissociated, denied or turned against oneself, though destructiveness of different sorts.

Briefly:

1. Early relational trauma must be recovered and received bodily by the therapist, and systems need to be reworked and circuits reactivated in the direction of healthy regulation. This can be done only through the active circuits of gaze–voice–face–body reconnection, mostly right brain based, as it is the amygdala in the right brain that has been most damaged and is also the seat of implicit memory and encoding. Contact between the two right brains can be reactivated only face to face, through the bodily connections through tuning and containment. This is why the therapist sometimes has physical symptoms while in the presence of certain patients, for instance, feeling dizzy, confused, sleepy, with physical pain such as a headache that vanishes after the patient leaves or nausea when the patient is retelling a particularly painful or horrendous story from the past. This is the abreactive part and is done through the presence of the body–mind–brain of the therapist,

which I have termed embodied testimony, and
which is mostly right brain based.

2. The traumatic residue needs to be released,
   re-elaborated and changed and, in place of a
   memory trace, a good relational experience needs
   to be introduced. This is mostly active reparation
   and re-inscription of a new reparatory experience:
   as Ferenczi said as early as 1932, 'abreaction is not
   enough'. And the active presence of the therapist
   is required. Through his or her embodied and
   committed witnessing, the therapist goes from right
   brain to left to right again.

Contrary to Freud's explanation (going back as early as
Studies on Hysteria) that the more the patient could abreact
(release the negative effect through the talking cure), the more
she could remember of the traumatic past and, as a result, the
more likely it was that symptoms would disappear, Ferenczi
underlined precisely what we believe today, that *abreaction is
not enough* if there has not been a truly relational reparative
experience: 'What is fundamentally significant in all this is the
fact that an abreaction of quantities of trauma is not enough;
the situation must be different from the actually traumatic
one in order to make possible a different, favourable outcome'
(Ferenczi, 1932a, p. 108).

In therapy, both partners extend the limits of their own experience and continually provoke a movement toward embodiment of new relational and intersubjective experiences, reparative of the old ones. It is not only a cognitive and social process but also a re-inscription of the bodily perception of one's self and one's body. It should be visible *in the body* as well as at the end of the treatment as the effect of a mirroring that has taken in parts of the interoceptive as well as exteroceptive perceptions of the two in the connection. I would not recommend working with individuals for whom we cannot feel empathy or sympathy, or at least for their life stories. If we are not capable of imagining the difficulties of the (now adult) patient with his or her own parent or caregiver with a sense of empathy, or simply in their own past circumstances, it is not a good omen for the clinical work.

The interactive process of mirroring through the gaze and the benevolent presence of the therapist, especially in the first phase when it is necessary to form an alliance, goes in the direction of creating soothing and emotional exchanges in accordance with the emotional fulfilment that is fundamental for emotional and affective growth and good development, as indicated by the classic studies carried out by Harlow, who showed how rhesus monkeys preferred the 'soft' caring mother to the metal frame providing milk. As Fairbairn (1952) has highlighted, what human beings need is the relationship more than the satisfaction of the bodily drive *per se*.

To summarize, several factors intervene in the definition of the 'meaning of trauma' and therefore in the level of traumatization, affecting the subtle threshold between internal and external.

- The presence or absence of an attachment figure, either as a participant in the event or as a source of comfort; to assist or to be involved in the trauma or in the death of a figure of attachment is equal to having been exposed personally to the event.
- The quality of attachment; to have a secure, insecure, disorganized attachment style changes the way we respond to the event.
- The social or cultural meaning assigned to the event and the subject's sharing of those cultural values.
- The presence or absence of relationships that can function socially and personally as cushions around the traumatized person.
- The length of time and the severity of the exposure to the event, and the age of the survivor at the time of the event.

And, to sum up, I would like to say that being resilient means:

1. That we have the capacity to love and trust (ourselves and others) through attachment because we have been loved and trusted.
2. That we are capable of remembering and honouring the living and the dead.
3. That we are linked through a network of symbolic, relational and cultural connectedness, ensuring the creation of meaning as individual and social threads.
4. That we belong to, cultivate and contribute to a network of education and cultural heritage in order to repair collective trauma.
5. That we take part in a celebration of the sacredness of life.
6. That we contribute, even without actual awareness but implicitly, to practices resulting in the care and love of the Earth and cherishing and cultivating what we have received.
7. That we are capable and constantly contribute to an intergenerational cycle of giving testimony and bearing witness, even in the practice of therapy as I understand it.

Finally, on the possibility of redemption of traumatic social dynamics, I would like to quote Gabriele Schwab (2010, p. 147):

> 'A culture that embraces the dehumanization
> of enemies is also vulnerable to a politics of
> revenge and retribution. By contrast, a mourning
> (and redress) that deserves its name requires an
> imaginative and affective practice that can only
> come from within an opposition to such culture.'

We need to maintain imaginative and affective practices and constant ways to create them.

BIBLIOGRAPHY

Abraham, N. and Torok, M. (1994). *The Shell and the Kernel: Renewals of Psychoanalysis* (Vol. 1). Chicago, IL: University of Chicago Press.

Akhtar, S. (1992) *Broken Structures: Severe Personality Disorders and their Treatment.* Northvale, NJ: Jason Aronson.

Akhtar, S. (1994) 'Object constancy and adult psychopathology'. *International Journal of psychoanalysis*, 75:441-455.

Akhtar, S. (2003) 'Dehumanization: origins, manifestations, and remedies' in: S. Varvin and V.D. Volkan. (eds.) Violence or Dialogues? Psychoanalytic Insights in Terror and Terrorism. London: International Psychoanalytic Association.

Akhtar, S. (2011) *Matters of Life and Death. Psychoanalytic Reflections.* London and New York: Routledge.

Akhtar, S. (2014) *Sources of Suffering. Fear, Greed, Guilt, Deception, Betrayal, and Revenge.* London and New York: Routledge.

Akhtar, S. (ed.) (2019) *Loss. Developmental, Cultural, and Clinical Realms.* London and New York: Routledge.

Amery, Jean. (1980) *At the Mind's Limits: Contemplations by a survivor on Auschwitz and its realities.* Bloomington, IN: Indiana University Press.

Anders, T.F. & Zeanah, C.H. (1984) 'Early infant development from a biological point of view', In J.D. Call, E. Galenson & R.L.Tyson (eds.) in Frontiers of Infant Psychiatry, vol. 2 (pp.55-69). New York: Basic Books.

American Psychiatric Association (2013) Diagnostic and Statistical Manual of Mental Disorders: DSM-5. Thailand: American Psychiatric Association.

Aron, L. (1996) *A meeting of the minds: mutuality of psychoanalysis.* Hillsdale, NJ: Analytic Press.

Auerhahn, N. C., and Laub, D. (1998). 'The primal scene of atrocity: The dynamic interplay between knowledge and fantasy of the Holocaust in children of survivors'. *Psychoanalytic Psychology*, 15(3), 360-377.

Barel, E., Van Ijzendoorn, M. H., Sagi-Schwartz, A. and Bakermans-Kranenburg, M. J. (2010). 'Surviving the Holocaust: A meta-analysis of the long-term sequelae of a genocide'. *Psychological Bulletin*, 136(5), 677-698.

Barnes, C.A., Eriksson, C.A., Davis, S. and McNaughton, B.L. (1995). 'Hippocampal synaptic enhancement as a basis for learning and memory: A selected review of current evidence from behaving animals'. In: J.L. McGaugh, N.M. Weinberger and

Bibliography

G. Lynch (eds), *Brain and Memory: Modulation and Mediation of Neuroplasticity*. Oxford and New York: Oxford University Press.

Barocas, H. A. and Barocas, C. B. (1980). 'Separation-individuation conflicts in children of Holocaust survivors'. Journal of Contemporary Psychotherapy, 11(1), 6–14.

Bar-On, D., Eland, J., Kleber, R. J., Krell, R., Moore, Y., Sagi, A. and van Ijzendoorn, M. H. (1998). 'Multigenerational perspectives on coping with the Holocaust experience: An attachment perspective for understanding the developmental sequelae of trauma across generations'. *International Journal of Behavioral Development*, 22(2), 315–38.

Baron-Cohen, S. (2011). *Zero Degrees of Empathy: A new theory of human cruelty*. London: Penguin.

Bateman, A. W. and Fonagy, P. (2004). 'Mentalization-based treatment of BPD'. *Journal of Personality Disorders*, 18(1), 36–51.

Benjamin, J (2018). *Beyond Doer and Done to: Recognition theory, intersubjectivity and the third*. New York: Pantheon Books.

Benjamin, J, (2004) Beyond doer and done to: an intersubjective view of thirdness. *Psychoanalytic Quarterly*, 73(1), 5-46.

Bollas, C. (1987). *The Shadow of the Object (Psychoanalysis of the Unthought Known)*. London : Free Association Books.

Borgogno, F. (2006). 'Thoughts on trauma in Ferenczi. A clinical-theoretical introduction'. In Bonomi, C. (ed.), *Sandor Ferenczi and contemporary psychoanalysis: Materials from the HS Sullivan Institute*, Florence, Rome: Borla.

Bowlby, J. (1969). *Attachment and Loss: Attachment* (Vol. 1). New York: Basic Books.

Bowlby, J. (1973). *Anger, Attachment and Loss: Separation, anxiety and anger*, Vol.2. New York: Basic Books.

Bradshaw, G. A., and Schore, A. N. (2007). 'How elephants are opening doors: Developmental neuroethology, attachment and social context'. *Ethology.*, 113(5), 426–36.

Bromberg, P. M. (2011). *The Shadow of the Tsunami: And the growth of the relational mind*. New York: Routledge.

Butler, J. (2004). *Precarious Life: The powers of violence and mourning*. London: Verso.

Carlson, V., Cicchetti, D., Barnett, D. and Braunwald, K. (1989). 'Disorganized/disoriented attachment relationships in maltreated infants'. *Developmental Psychology*, 25(4), 525.

Caruth, C. (1996). *Unclaimed Experience: Trauma, Narrative, and History*. Baltimore and London: Johns Hopkins University Press.

Caruth, C. (2014). *Listening to Trauma: Conversations with leaders in the theory and treatment of catastrophic experience*. Baltimore, MA: Johns Hopkins University Press.

Cicchetti, D., Rogosh, F. A., and Tosh, S. (2006). 'Fostering secure attachment in infants in maltreating families through preventing interventions'. *Development and Psychopathology*, 18, 623–60.

Cozolino, L. (2002). *The Neuroscience of Psychotherapy: Building and rebuilding the human brain* (Norton Series on Interpersonal Neurobiology). New York: WW Norton.

Cozolino, L. (2006). *The Neuroscience of Human Relationships: Attachment and the developing social brain* (Norton Series on Interpersonal Neurobiology). New York: WW Norton.

Damasio, A.R. (1999) *The feeling of what happens: Body and Emotions in the Making of Consciousness,* New York, NY: Hartcourt Brace.

Danieli, Y. (1981). 'Differing adaptational styles in families of survivors of the Nazi Holocaust'. Children Today, 10(5), 6-10.

Danieli, Y. (ed.) (1998) International Handbook of Multigenerational Legacies of Trauma. New York and London: Plenum Press.

De Bellis, M. D. (2001). 'Developmental traumatology: The psychobiological development of maltreated children and its implications for research, treatment and policy'. *Development and Psychopathology*, 13, 539–64.

Dell, P.F. and O'Neill, J.A. (eds) (2009). *Dissociation and the Dissociative Disorders: DSM-IV and Beyond.* New York: Routledge.

De Zulueta, F. (2006). *From Pain to Violence: The traumatic roots of destructiveness.* New York: Wiley.

Diamond, D. (2004) 'Attachment disorganization: The reunion of attachment theory and psychoanalysis'. *Psychoanalytic Psychology,* 21 (2), 276-289.

Diamond, D, Clarkin, J.F.Levy, K.N., Levine, H., and Foelsch, P. (2002) 'The Clinical implications of current attachment research for interventions with borderline patients'. *Journal of Infant, Child, and Adolescent Psychotherapy*, 2(4): 121-149.

Diamond, D., Draijer, N. and Langeland, W. (1999). 'Childhood trauma and perceived parental dysfunction in the etiology of dissociative symptoms in psychiatric inpatients'. *American Journal of Psychiatry*, 156(3), 379–85.

Edelman, G. M. (1987). *Neural Darwinism.* New York: Basic Books.

Eisenberg, L. (1995). 'The social construction of the human brain'. *American Journal of Psychiatry*, 152(11), 1563–75.

Eitinger, L. (1961). 'Pathology of the concentration camp syndrome: Preliminary report'. *Archives of General Psychiatry*, 5(4), 371–9.

Eriksson, P. S., Perfilieva, E., Björk-Eriksson, T., Alborn, A. M., Nordborg, C., Peterson, D. A. and Gage, F. H. (1998). 'Neurogenesis in the adult human hippocampus'. *Nature Medicine*, 4(11), 1313–17.

Fairnbairn, R.G. (1952) *Psychoanalytical Studies of Personality.* New York: Routledge.

Bibliography

Felitti, V.J, Anda, R.F., (2010). 'The relationship of adverse childhood experiences to adult medical disease, psychiatric disorders and sexual behavior. Implications for healthcare'. In Lanius, R. A., Vermetten, E., Pain, C., (eds.) *The Impact of Early Life Trauma on Health and Disease: The Hidden Epidemic*. Cambridge, UK: Cambridge University Press.

Felsen, I. (1998). 'Transgenerational Transmission of Effects of the Holocaust'. In Y. Danieli, (ed.), *International Handbook of Multigenerational Legacies of Trauma* (pp. 43–68). Boston, MA: Springer.

Ferenczi, S. (1929). 'The unwelcome child and his death instinct'. *International Journal of Psychoanalysis*, 10: 125–29.

Ferenczi, C. (1932a). *The Clinical Diary of Sandor Ferenczi* (ed. E. Dupont). Cambridge, MA and London: Harvard University Press, 1988.

Ferenczi, S. (1932b). 'Confusion of tongues between adults and the child'. Paper read before the International Psychoanalytic Congress. Wiesbaden.

Fonagy, P. (2000). 'Attachment and borderline personality disorder'. *Journal of the American Psychoanalytic Association*, 48(4), 1129–46.

Fonagy, P. and Target, M. (2002). 'Fathers in Modern Psychoanalysis and in Society: The role of the father and child development'. In: J. Trowell and A. Etchegoyen (eds.), *The Importance of Fathers. The New Library of Psychoanalysis*, 42, 45–66. East Sussex: Brunner-Routledge.

Fonagy, P., Moran, G., Steele, M. and Steele, H. (1992). *The integration of psychoanalytic theory and the work of attachment: the intergenerational perspective*. Rome: Laterza.

Fonagy, P., Target, M., Gergely, G., Allen, J. G., and Bateman, A. W. (2003). 'The developmental roots of borderline personality disorder in early attachment relationships: A theory and some evidence'. *Psychoanalytic Inquiry*, 23(3), 412–59.

Fonagy, P., Gergely, G., Jurist, E. L. and Target, M. (2004). *Affect Regulation, Mentalization and the Development of the Self*. New York: Other Press.

Frankel, J. B. (2011). 'Ferenczi's concept of identification with the aggressor and play as foundational processes in the analytic relationship'. In A. A. Druck, C. Ellman, N. Freedman and A. Thaler (eds.), *A New Freudian Synthesis*. (pp. 173–200). London: Karnac Books.

Freud, S. (1917/1953). 'Mourning and melancholia'. In J. Strachey (ed. and trans.), *The Standard Edition of the Complete Psychological Works of Sigmund Freud* (Vol. 14, pp. 237–58). London: Hogarth Press.

Freud, S. (1918).From the history of an infantile neurosis: SE Vol XVII (1917-1919). *An Infantile Neurosis and Other works*. (pp 1-124).

Freud, S. (1920/1953). 'Beyond the pleasure principle'. In J. Strachey (ed. and trans.), *The

Standard Edition of the Complete Psychological Works of Sigmund Freud (Vol. 18, pp. 1–64). London: Hogarth Press.

George, C., and Main, M. (1979). 'Social interactions of young abused children: Approach, avoidance and aggression.' *Child Development*, 50, 306–18

Gergely, G. (1992). 'Developmental reconstructions: Infancy from the point of view of psychoanalysis and developmental psychology.' *Psychoanalysis and Contemporary Thought*, 15(1): 3–55.

Gerson, S. (2009). 'When the third is dead: Memory, mourning, and witnessing in the aftermath of the Holocaust.' *International Journal of Psychoanalysis*, 90(6), 1341–57.

Green, A. (1993). 'The dead mother.' *Psyche*, 47(3), 205–40.

Green, A. (2004) "Thirdness and psychoanalytic concepts". *The Psychoanalytic Quarterly*, 73(1): 99-135

Gross, C. G. (2000). 'Neurogenesis in the Adult Brain: Death of a dogma.' *Nature Reviews Neuroscience*, 1(1), 67–73.

Grubrich-Simitis, I. (1981). 'Extreme traumatization as cumulative trauma: Psychoanalytic investigations of the effects of concentration camp experiences on survivors and their children.' *The Psychoanalytic Study of the Child*, 36(1), 415–50.

Harris, A., Kalb, M., and Klebanoff, S. (2017) (eds.) *Ghosts in the Consulting Room. Echoes of Trauma in psychoanalysis.* London and New York: Routledge.

Harris, A., Kalb, M., and Klebanoff, S. (2017) (eds.) *Demons in the Consulting Room. Echoes of Genocide, slavery and extreme trauma in psychoanalytic practice.* London and New York: Routledge.

Henry, J.P. (1993). 'Psychological and physiological responses to stress: The right hemisphere and the hypothalamo-pituitary-adrenal axis, an inquiry into problems of human bonding.' *Integrative Physiological and Behavioral Science*, 28, 369–87.

Hesse, E. and Main, M. (2006). 'Frightened, threatening, and dissociative parental behavior in low-risk samples: Description, discussion, and interpretations.' *Development and Psychopathology*, 18(2), 309–43.

Hobfoll, S. E. and London, P. (1986). 'The Relationship of self-concept and social support to emotional distress Among Women During War.' *Journal of Social and Clinical Psychology*, 4(2), 189–203.

Hockfield, S. and Lombroso, P. J. (1998). 'Development of the cerebral cortex: X. Cortical development and experience: II.' *Journal of the American Academy of Child and Adolescent Psychiatry*, 37(10), 1103–5.

Hofer, M.A. (1994). 'Hidden regulators in attachment, separation, and loss.' *Monographs of the Society for Research in Child Development*, 59 (1–2):

Hoffman, Y. and Shrira, A. (2019). 'Variables connecting parental ptsd to offspring suc-

Bibliography

cessful aging: Parent–child role reversal, secondary traumatization, and depressive symptoms'. *Frontiers in Psychiatry*, 10, 718.

Hugdahl, K. (1995). *Psychophysiology: The mind–body perspective*. Cambridge, MA: Harvard University Press.

Joseph, R. (1996). *Neuropsychiatry, Neuropsychology, and Clinical Neuroscience: Emotion, evolution, cognition, language, memory, brain damage, and abnormal behavior*. Philadelphia, PA: Williams & Wilkins.

Kandel, E. R. (1999). 'Biology and the future of psychoanalysis: A new intellectual framework for psychiatry revisited'. *American Journal of Psychiatry*, 156(4), 505–24.

Kempermann, G., Kuhn, H.G. and Gage, F.H. (1997). 'More hippocampal neurons in mice living in an enriched environment'. *Nature*, 386: 493–5.

Kernberg O. F. (1975). *Borderline Conditions and Pathological Narcissism*. New York: Aronson.

Kernberg, O. F. (2004). *Aggressivity, Narcissism and Self-destructiveness in the Psychotherapeutic Relationship: New Developments in the Psychopathology and Psychotherapy of Severe personality Disorders*. New Haven, CT: Yale University Press.

Kirshner, L. A. (1994). 'Trauma, the good object, and the symbolic: A theoretical integration'. *International Journal of Psychoanalysis*, 75, 235–42.

Kochanska, G. (2001). 'Emotional Development in Children with Different Attachment Histories: The first three years'. *Child Development*, 72(2), 474–90.

Krystal, H. (ed.), (1968). *Massive Psychic Trauma*. New York: International Universities Press.

Langer, E. J. (1989). 'Minding matters: The consequences of mindlessness–mindfulness'. In *Advances in Experimental Social Psychology*, 22: 137–73.

Laub, D. (1992). 'Bearing witness or the vicissitudes of listening'. In S. Felman, and D. Laub (eds), *Testimony: Crises of witnessing in literature, psychoanalysis, and history*, pp. 57–74. New York and London: Routledge.

Laub, D. (2005a) Traumatic shutdown of narrative and symbolization: A death instinct derivative? *Contemporary Psychoanalysis*, 41: 307-326.

Laub, D. (2005b). 'From speechlessness to narrative: The cases of Holocaust historians and of psychiatrically hospitalized survivors'. *Literature and Medicine*, 24, 253–65.

Laub, D., and Auerhahn, N. C. (1984). 'Reverberations of genocide: Its expression in the conscious and unconscious of post-Holocaust generations'. *Psychoanalytic Reflections on the Holocaust*, 151–67. New York.

Laub, D. and Auerhahn, N. C. (1989). 'Failed empathy: A central theme in the survivor's

Holocaust experience'. *Psychoanalytic Psychology*, 6(4), 377.

Laub, D. and Auerhahn, N. C. (1993). 'Knowing and not knowing massive psychic trauma: Forms of traumatic memory'. *International Journal of Psychoanalysis*, 74, 287 302.

Laub, D. and Lee, S. (2003). 'Thanatos and massive psychic trauma: The impact of the death instinct on knowing, remembering, and forgetting'. *Journal of the American Psychoanalytic Association*, 51(2), 433–64.

Lemma, A. (2010). *Under the Skin: A psychoanalytic study of body modification*. London: Routledge.

Levi, P. (1996). *If this is a Man* [known as *Survival in Auschwitz* in the USA]. London: Simon & Schuster.

Levi, P. (2017). *The Drowned and the Saved*. London: Simon & Schuster.

Lev-Wiesel, R. (2007). 'Intergenerational transmission of trauma across three generations: A preliminary study'. *Qualitative Social Work*, 6(1), 75–94.

Linden, D. E. J. (2006). 'How Psychotherapy Changes The Brain: The contribution of functional neuroimaging'. *Molecular Psychiatry*, 11(6), 528–38.

Lingiardi, V. and McWilliams, N. (eds) (2017). *Psychodynamic Diagnostic Manual*, 2nd edn. New York and London: Guilford Press.

Liotti, G. (1992). 'Disorganization of attachment and vulnerability to the development of functional disorders of consciousness'. In M. Ammaniti and D. N. Stern (ed), *Attachment and Psychoanalysis* (pp. 219–32). Rome: Laterza.

Liotti, G. (1992b). 'Disorganized/disoriented attachment in the psychotherapy of the dissociative disorders'. Dissociation 4:196-204.

Liotti, G. (2004). 'Trauma, dissociation, and disorganized attachment: Three strands of a single braid'. *Psychotherapy: Theory, research, practice, training*, 41(4), 472.

Liotti, G. (2005). 'Trauma e dissociazione alla luce della teoria dell'attaccamento'. *Infanzia e Adolescenza*, 4(3), 130–44.

Liotti, G., and Farina, B. (2011). *Traumatic Developments: Etiopathogenesis, clinical reflections and treatment of the dissociative dimension*. Milan: Raffaello Cortina Editions.

Liotti, G., Intreccialagli, B., and Cerere, F. (1991). 'The experience of mourning in the mother and facilitation to the development of dissociative disorders in the consciousness of the offspring. A control-case study'. *Journal of Psychiatry*, 26, 283–91.

Lyons-Ruth, K. (2003). 'Dissociation and the parent–infant dialogue: A longitudinal perspective from attachment research'. *Journal of the American Psychoanalytic Association*, 51, 883–911.

Lyons-Ruth, K., Bronfman, E., and Atwood, G. (1999). 'A relational diathesis model

Bibliography

of hostile-helpless states of mind: Expressions in mother–infant interaction'. In J. Solomon and C. George (eds), *Attachment Disorganization* (pp. 33–70). New York: Guilford Press.

Lyons-Ruth, K., Zoll, D., Connell, D. and Odom, R. (1987). 'Maternal depression as mediator of the effects of home-based intervention services'. In *Abstracts of Bi-Annual meeting of Society for Research in Child Development* Vol. 7, p. 189.

Lyons-Ruth, K., Connell, D. B., Grunebaum, H. U. and Botein, S. (1990). 'Infants at social risk: Maternal depression and family support services as mediators of infant development and security of attachment'. *Child Development*, 61(1), 85–98.

Lyons-Ruth, K., and Jacobvitz, D. (1999). 'Attachment disorganization: Unresolved loss, relational violence, and lapses in behavioral and attentional strategies'. In J. Cassidy and P. R. Shaver (eds), *Handbook of Attachment: Theory, research, and clinical applications* (pp. 520–54). New York: Guilford Press.

McCann, I. L., and Pearlman, L. A. (1990). *Psychological Trauma and the Adult Survivor: Theory, therapy, and transformation*, No. 21. London: Psychology Press.

MacLean, P. D. (1990). *The Triune Brain in Evolution: Role in paleocerebral functions*. New York: Springer Science and Business Media.

Maffei, L. (2011). *The Freedom to Be Different. Nature and Culture at the Trial of Neuroscience*. Bologna: Il Mulino.

Maloney, L. J. (1988). 'Post-traumatic stresses on women partners of Vietnam veterans'. *Smith College Studies in Social Work*, 58(2), 122–43.

Mancia, M. (2006). 'Implicit memory and early unrepressed unconscious: Their role in the therapeutic process (how the neurosciences can contribute to psychoanalysis'. *International Journal of Psychoanalysis*, 87(Part 1), 83–103.

Markowitsch, H. J., Thiel, A., Reinkemeier, M., Kessler, J., Koyuncu, A., and Heiss, W. D. (2000). 'Right amygdala and temporofrontal activation during autobiographic, but not during fictitious memory retrieval'. *Behavioural Neurology*, 12(4), 181–90.

Martens, W. H. (2000). 'Antisocial and psychopathic personality disorders: Causes, course, and remission: A review article'. *International Journal of Offender Therapy and Comparative Criminology*, 44(4), 406–30.

McDougall, J. (1989). *Theatres of the Body: A psychoanalytic approach to psychosomatic illness*. New York: WW Norton.

Meaney, M. J. (2001). 'Maternal care, gene expression, and the transmission of individual differences in stress reactivity across generations'. *Annual Review of Neuroscience*, 24(1), 1161–92.

Mészáros, J. (2014, January). 'Ferenczi's "wise baby" phenomenon and resilience'. *International Forum of Psychoanalysis*, 23 (1), 3–10).

Mitchell, S. A. (1988). *Relational Concepts in Psychoanalysis. An Integration*. Cambridge, MA: Harvard University Press.

Mucci, C. (2008). *Extreme Sorrow: Trauma from Freud to the Shoah*. Roma: Borla.

Mucci, C. (2013). *Beyond Individual and Collective Trauma: Intergenerational transmission, psychoanalytic treatment, and the dynamics of forgiveness*. London: Karnac Books.

Mucci, C. (2018a). *Borderline Bodies: Affect Regulation Therapy for Personality Disorders (Norton Series on Interpersonal Neurobiology)*. New York: WW Norton and Company.

Mucci, C. (2018b). 'Psychoanalysis for a new humanism: Embodied testimony, connectedness, memory and forgiveness for a "persistence of the human"'. *International Forum of Psychoanalysis*. 27 (3), 176–87.

Mucci, C. (2019) in Akhtar, S. (ed.) 'Loss as the Relational Basis of the Self and the Politics of Mourning'. In Akhtar,s. (2019) (Ed.). *Loss. Developmental, Cultural, and Clinical Realms*. New York: Routledge.

Mucci, C. (2021a). 'A right-brain dissociative model for right-brain disorders: Dissociation vs repression in borderline and other severe psychopathologies of early traumatic origin'. In *The Divided Therapist*, pp. 202–27. London and New York: Routledge.

Mucci, C. (2021b) Dissociation vs Repression: a New Psychoanalytic Model for Psychopathology. *The American Journal of Psychoanalysis,* 81:82-111.

Mucci, C., Scalabrini, A. (2021) Traumatic effects beyond diagnosis: The impact of dissociation on the mind–body–brain system. *Psychoanalytic Psychology*, 20 38.4: 279.

Murphy, A., Steele, M., Dube, S.R., Bate, J., Bonuck, K, Meissner, P. and Steele, H. (2014). Adverse Childhood Experiences (ACEs) questionnaire and adult attachment interview (AAI): implications for parent-child relationships. Child abuse & neglect, 38(2): 224-233.

Narvaez, D., Panksepp, J., Schore, A., and Gleason, T. (2013). *Evolution, Early Experience and Human Development: From research to practice and policy*. New York: Oxford University Press.

Nelson, E. E. and Panksepp, J. (1998). 'Brain substrates of infant–mother attachment: Contributions of opioids, oxytocin, and norepinephrine'. *Neuroscience and Biobehavioral Reviews*, 22(3), 437–52.

Niederland, W. G. (1968). 'Clinical observations on the "survivor syndrome"'. *International Journal of Psycho-Analysis*, 49, 313–15.

Niederland, W.G. (1981). 'The survivor syndrome: Further observations and dimensions'. *Journal of the American Psychoanalytic Association*, 29: 413–25.

Ogden, T. (2004). The analytic third: Implications for psychoanalytic theory and tech-

Bibliography

nique. *Psychoanalytic Quarterly,* 73(1): 167-195.

Ornstein, A. (2004). *My Mother's Eyes: Holocaust memories of a young girl.* Covington, KY: Clerisy Press, Emmis Books.

Panksepp, J. and Biven, E. (2012). 'A meditation on the affective neuroscientific view of human and animalian mind–brains'. In A. Fotopoulou, D. Pfaff, and M.A. Conway (ed.), From the couch to the lab: Trends in psychodynamic neuroscience, (pp. 145–75). Oxford University Press.

Paris, J. and Zweig-Frank, H. (1997). 'Dissociation in patients with borderline personality disorder'. *American Journal of Psychiatry,* 154, 137–38.

Paris, J. and Zweig-Frank, H. (2001). 'A 27-year follow-up of patients with borderline personality disorder'. *Comprehensive Psychiatry,* 42(6), 482–87.

Perry, B. D., Pollard, R. A., Blakley, T. L., Baker, W. L. and Vigilante, D. (1995). 'Childhood trauma, the neurobiology of adaptation, and use dependent development of the brain: How state become traits'. *Infant Mental Health Journal,* 16(4): 271–91.

Pianta, R. C., Egeland, B. and Sroufe, L. A. (1990). 'Maternal stress and children's development: Prediction of school outcomes and identification of protective factors'. *Risk and Protective Factors in the Development of Psychopathology,* 215–35.

Porges, S. W. (2011). *The Polyvagal Theory: Neurophysiological foundations of emotions, attachment, communication, and self-regulation* (Norton Series on Interpersonal Neurobiology). New York: WW Norton and Company.

Rachman, A. W. and Klett, S. (2015). *Analysis of the Incest Trauma. Retrieval, recovery, renewal.* London: Karnac Books.

Rachman, A, and Mucci, C. (2022). *Confusion of Tongues Trauma Theory.* New York: Routledge.

Rakoff, V., Sigal, J. J. and Epstein, N. B. (1966). 'Children and families of concentration camp survivors'. *Canada's Mental Health,* 14(4), 24–6.

Reddy, V. (2008). *How Infants Know Minds.* Cambridge, MA: Harvard University Press.

Roelofs, K., Keijsers, G. P., Hoogduin, K. A., Näring, G. W. and Moene, F. C. (2002). Childhood 'abuse in patients with conversion disorder'. *American Journal of Psychiatry,* 159(11), 1908–13.

Rosenheck, R. and Nathan, P. (1985). 'Secondary traumatization in children of Vietnam veterans'. *Psychiatric Services,* 36(5), 538–39.

Sagi, A., Van Ijzendoorn, M. H., Joels, T. and Scharf, M. (2002). 'Disorganized reasoning in Holocaust survivors'. *American Journal of Orthopsychiatry,* 72(2), 194–203.

Sagi-Schwartz, Koren-Karie, N. and Joels T. (2003) 'Failed Mourning in the Adult Attachment Interview: The case of Holocaust child survivors'. Attachment and Human development, 5: 398-409.

Sagi-Schwartz, A., van Ijzendoorn, M. H. and Bakermans-Kranenburg, M. J. (2008). 'Does intergenerational transmission of trauma skip a generation? No meta-analytic evidence for tertiary traumatization with third generation of Holocaust survivors'. *Attachment and Human Development*, 10(2), 105–21.

Sagi-Schwartz, A., van IJzendoorn, M. H., Grossmann, K. E., Joels, T., Grossmann, K., Scharf, M. and Alkalay, S. (2003). 'Attachment and traumatic stress in female holocaust child survivors and their daughters'. *American Journal of Psychiatry*, 160(6), 1086–92.

Sapolsky, R. (2017). *Behave. The biology of humans at our best and worst.* London: Vintage.

Scalabrini, A., Mucci, C., Esposito, R., Daminai, S. and Northoff, G. (2020) Dissociation as a disorder of integration. On the footsteps of Pierre Janet. *Progress in Neuropharmacology and Biological Psychiatry*, 101, 1099928. ISO 69.

Scharf, M. and Mayseless, O. (2011). 'Disorganizing experiences in second- and third-generation Holocaust survivors'. *Qualitative Health Research*, 21(11), 1539–53.

Schiffer, F., Teicher, M. H. and Papanicolaou, A. C. (1995). 'Evoked potential evidence for right brain activity during the recall of traumatic memories'. *Journal of Neuropsychiatry and Clinical Neurosciences*, 7 (2), 169–175.

Schore, A. N. (1994). *Affect Regulation and the Origin of the Self: The neurobiology of emotional development.* Mahwah, NJ: Erlbaum.

Schore, A. N. (2001a). 'The effects of a secure attachment relationship on right brain development, affect regulation, and infant mental health'. *Infant Mental Health Journal*, 22, 7–66.

Schore, A. N. (2001b). 'The effects of early relational trauma on right brain development, affect regulation, and infant mental health'. *Infant Mental Health Journal*, 22(1–2), 201–69.

Schore, A. N. (2002). 'Dysregulation of the right brain: A fundamental mechanism of traumatic attachment and the psychopathogenesis of posttraumatic stress disorder'. *Australian and New Zealand Journal of Psychiatry*, 36(1), 9–30.

Schore, A. N. (2003a). *Affect Regulation and the Repair of the Self.* New York: Norton.

Schore, A. N. (2003b). *Affect Dysregulation and Disorders of the Self.* New York: Norton.

Schore, A. N. (2010). 'Relational trauma and the developing right brain: The neurobiology of broken attachment bonds'. In T. Baradon (ed.), *Relational Trauma in Infancy: Psychoanalytic, attachment and neuropsychological contributions to parent–infant psychotherapy* (pp. 19–47). London: Routledge/Taylor & Francis Group.

Schore, A. N. (2012). *The Science of the Art of Psychotherapy (Norton Series on*

Bibliography

Interpersonal Neurobiology). New York: Norton.

Schore, A. N. (2016). 'The right brain implicit self: A central mechanism of the psycho-therapy change process'. In G. Craparo and C. Mucci (eds), *Unrepressed Unconscious, Implicit Memory, and Clinical Work* (pp. 73–98). London: Karnac Books.

Schore, A. N. (2017). 'All our sons: The developmental neurobiology and neuroendocrinology of boys at risk'. *Infant Mental Health*, 38(1), 15–52.

Schore, A.N. (2019a) *The Development of the Unconscious Mind*. New York: W.W. Norton.

Schore, A. N. (2019b) *Right Brain Psychotherapy*. New York: W.W. Norton.

Schwab, G. (2010). *Haunting Legacies: Violent Histories and Transgenerational Trauma*. New York: Columbia University Press.

Shmotkin, D., Shrira, A., Goldberg, S. C. and Palgi, Y. (2011). 'Resilience and vulnerability among aging Holocaust survivors and their families: An intergenerational overview'. *Journal of Intergenerational Relationships*, 9(1), 7–21.

Siegel, D. J. (1999). *The Developing Mind*. New York: Guilford Press.

Solomon, Z., Kotler, M. and Mikulincer, M. (1988). 'Combat-related post-traumatic stress disorder among second-generation Holocaust survivors: Preliminary findings'. *The American Journal of Psychiatry*, 145: 865-868.

Solomon, S.D., Gerrity, E.T. and Alyson M. Muff. 'Efficacy of treatments for posttraumatic stress disorder: An empirical review'. *JAMA*, 268(5), 633–8.

Sroufe, L. A. (1997). 'Psychopathology as an outcome of development'. Development and Psychopathology, 9(2), 251–68.

Sroufe, L. A., Egeland, B. and Kreutzer, T. (1990). 'The fate of early experience following developmental change: Longitudinal approaches to individual adaptation in childhood'. *Child Development*, 61(5), 1363–73.

Steele, H. and Siever, L. (2010) 'An attachment perspective on borderline personality disorder: Advances in gene-environment considerations'. *Current Psychiatry Reports*, 12 (1): 61-67.

Steele, H. and Steele, M. (eds.) (2017) *Handbook of attachment-based interventions*. New York: Guilford Press.

Steele, H. and Steele, M. (1998) Attachment and psychoanalysis: Time for a reunion. *Social development*, 7 (1): 92-119

Tomasello, M. (2019). *Becoming Human: A theory of ontogeny*. Harvard, MA: Belknap Press.

Trevarthen, C. (2005). Action and emotion in development of cultural intelligence: Why infants have feelings like ours. In J. Nadel and D. Muir, (eds.) *Emotional Development*, (61-91). Oxford: Oxford University Press.

Trevathan, W. R. (2011). *Human Birth: An evolutionary perspective*. London: Routledge.

Tronick, E. (2007). *The Neurobehavioral and Social–Emotional Development of Infants and Children*. New York: Norton.

Tronick, E., Als, H., Adamson, L., Wise, S. and Brazelton, T. B. (1978). 'The infant's response to entrapment between contradictory messages in face to face interaction'. *Journal of the American Academy of Child Psychiatry*, 17(1), 1–13.

Tucker, D. M. (1992). 'Developing emotions and cortical networks'. In M.R. Gunnar and C.A. Nelson (Eds). Minnesota Symposium on Child Psychology, Vol. 24. *Developmental Behavioral Neuroscience* (Vol. 24 pp. 75–128). Hillsdale, NJ: Erlbaum.

Tweedy, R. (2021) (ed.) *The Divided Therapist: Hemispheric Difference and Contemporary Psychotherapy*. London: Routledge.

Van der Kolk, B. (2014). *The Body Keeps the Score: Mind, brain and body in the transformation of trauma*. London: Penguin.

Van Ijzendoorn, M. H., Bakermans-Kranenburg, M. J. and Ebstein, R. P. (2011). 'Methylation matters in child development: Toward developmental behavioral epigenetics'. *Child Development Perspectives*, 5(4), 305–10.

Van Ijzendoorn, M. H., Bakermans-Kranenburg, M. J. and Sagi-Schwartz, A. (2003). 'Are children of Holocaust survivors less well-adapted? A meta-analytic investigation of secondary traumatization'. *Journal of Traumatic Stress*, 16(5), 459–69.

Van Ijzendoorn, M. H., Schuengel, C. and Bakermans-Kranenburg, M. J. (1999). 'Disorganized attachment in early childhood: Meta-analysis of precursors, concomitants, and sequelae'. *Development and Psychopathology*, 11, 225–49.

Wiesel, E. (1995). *All Rivers Run to the Sea: Memoirs*. New York: Alfred Knopf.

Wiesel, E. (2006). *Night* (trans. M. Wiesel). New York: Hill and Wang.

Wiesel, E. and Heffner, R.D. (2001). *Conversations with Elie Wiesel*. New York: Schocken Books.

Yehuda, R., Schmeidler, J., Weinberg, M., Binden-Bryner, K. and Duvdenani, T. (1998). 'Vulnerability to post-traumatic stress disorder in adult offspring of Holocaust survivors'. *American Journal of Psychiatry*, 155, 1163–71.

Yehuda, R., Bierer, L. M., Schmeidler, J., Aferiat, D. H., Breslau, I. and Dolan, S. (2000). 'Low cortisol and risk for PTSD in adult offspring of Holocaust survivors'. *American Journal of Psychiatry*, 157(8), 1252–59.

Yehuda, R., Daskalakis, N. P., Lehrner, A., Desarnaud, F., Bader, H. N., Makotkine, I. and Meaney, M. J. (2014). 'Influences of maternal and paternal PTSD on epigenetic regulation of the glucocorticoid receptor gene in Holocaust survivor offspring'. *American Journal of Psychiatry*, 171(8), 872–80.

Ziabreva, I., Poeggel, G., Schnabel, R. and Braun, K. (2003). 'Separation-induced receptor changes in the hippocampus and amygdala of *Octodon degus*: Influence of maternal vocalizations'. *Journal of Neuroscience*, 23(12), 5329–36.

INDEX

Index

Index

Index

Resilience and Survival

Index

Index

Resilience and Survival